# Pre-Raphaelite Women Artists

Jan Marsh & Pamela Gerrish Nunn

JAN MARSH AND PAMELA GERRISH NUNN

# Pre-Raphaelite Women Artists

*With 231 illustrations, 65 in color*

THAMES AND HUDSON

*Barbara Leigh Smith Bodichon*

*Anna Mary Howitt*

*Rosa Brett*

*Anna Eliza Blunden*

*Jane Benham Hay*

*Joanna Mary Boyce*

*Elizabeth Eleanor Siddal*

*Rebecca Solomon*

*Emma Sandys*

*Julia Margaret Cameron*

*Lucy Madox Brown*

*Catherine Madox Brown*

*Marie Spartali Stillman*

*Maria Cassavetti Zambaco*

*Francesca Alexander*

*Evelyn De Morgan*

*Kate Elizabeth Bunce*

*Marianne Preindelsberger Stokes*

*Christiana Jane Herringham*

*Eleanor Fortescue Brickdale*

This book was originally published on the occasion of the
exhibition *Pre-Raphaelite Women Artists* organized by Manchester
City Art Galleries. The exhibition was shown at Manchester City
Art Galleries, 22 November 1997 – 22 February 1998; at
Birmingham Museum and Art Gallery, 7 March – 25 May 1998;
and at Southampton City Art Gallery, 6 June – 2 August 1998.
Exhibition tour sponsored by Willis Corroon Fine Art

**WILLIS CORROON FINE ART** ◆◆◆

*Frontispiece: Eleanor Fortescue Brickdale* The Little Foot Page, *1905,
Board and Trustees of the National Museums on Merseyside
(Walker Art Gallery, Liverpool).*

Text © 1997 Manchester City Art Galleries and the authors
Reprinted 1998 by Thames and Hudson Ltd, London

First published in paperback in the United States of America in 1999 by
Thames and Hudson Inc., 500 Fifth Avenue, New York, New York 10110

Library of Congress Catalog Card Number 98-61449
ISBN 0-500-28104-1

Printed and bound in Italy

# Contents

# Foreword & Acknowledgements

The Pre-Raphaelite Brotherhood was established in 1848, a group of artists united by a concern for the truthful observation of nature, an interest in present day life and motivated by a strong sense of the moral purpose of art. The original Brotherhood was comparatively short-lived but from it developed a movement of many strands long known as Pre-Raphaelitism. Its spirit exerted a strong influence throughout the century, particularly through the Aesthetic and Arts and Crafts movements. In the 1960s, after an almost obligatory period of being out of fashion for decades, the Pre-Raphaelites were rehabilitated. Since then they would seem to have been exhaustively researched and widely exhibited. Today their popular appeal has probably never been greater, representing for many the high point of Victorian art. This interest has focused entirely on the male artists who by definition, constituted the Brotherhood, however loosely defined. As this exhibition sets out to show, this view has excluded an important body of work by women artists who can also claim to have followed the precepts of Pre-Raphaelitism.

It is remarkable that the achievements of many of the artists included in the exhibition should have remained obscured for so long. Their rediscovery and reassessment has been a personal mission for Pamela Gerrish Nunn and Jan Marsh, who conceived and selected the exhibition. I am grateful to them for the energy and expertise which they have contributed to the project. Their work has been an exploration, assiduously tracking down both artists and paintings. Important works have been rediscovered and several are receiving their first exhibition this century. From the extensive research of Pamela Gerrish Nunn and Jan Marsh a picture emerges of a movement which was significantly enriched by the hitherto neglected women artists who practised alongside their better-known male contemporaries. It is their achievement that the exhibition and this publication redefines the nature of Pre-Raphaelitism as we approach both the 150th anniversary of its founding and the centenary of the death of Edward Burne-Jones, the dominant force in the shaping of the movement's final period.

It is appropriate that Pre-Raphaelite Women Artists should be initiated by Manchester City Art Galleries: not only have we one of the finest collections of Pre-Raphaelite paintings in the country, but the north west region was an important source of patronage for these painters.

I am grateful to the many lenders to the exhibition, without whose support this survey would not have been possible. I particularly thank those private lenders who have lent their pictures for the extended loan period, thus enabling the exhibition to tour to Birmingham and Southampton.

The tour has been sponsored by Willis Corroon Fine Art. This is the second of our exhibitions to benefit from their sponsorship and I am grateful that Louise Hallett and Hugo Headlam responded so positively to our suggestion that they become involved. Their sponsorship has been matched by an award under the ABSA Pairing Scheme and our thanks are due to Chris Pulleine of ABSA North for his advice.

The Patrons of Manchester City Art Galleries have once again been generous benefactors to the Galleries by supporting this catalogue. The Paul Mellon Centre for Studies in British Art has also provided a grant, for which we are grateful.

Numerous individuals have offered assistance with all aspects of the exhibition and catalogue but Manchester City Art Galleries and the Selectors would particularly like to thank the following: the late Colin Bather, Martin Beisly, Mary Bennett, Mark Bills, Susan P. Casteras, Anne Christopherson, Sarah Colegrave, George Comenos and staff, John Crabbe, David Dallas, Dr. Simon Drachman, Betty Elzea, Magdalen Evans, Julia Findlater, Elree Harris, Julian Hartnoll, Michael Hickox, Jock Hopson, Lewis Hutchings, Dr. Catherine Gordon and the De Morgan Foundation, Veronique Gunner, Dr. Pam Hirsch, Jane Hollond, Alison Keating, Dr. Mary Lago, Rupert Maas, Sheila MacGregor, Mark Samuels Lasner, Tilly Marshall, David Mason, Edward Morris, Julia Nagle, Christopher Newall, Roderic O'Conor, Mr. & Mrs. Herbert Pell, Liz Prettejohn, John Purkis, William Ritchie, Mr. & Mrs. Charles Rossetti, Mrs. Vicky Scarborough, David and Oliver Soskice, Alistair Smith, Dr. M.G. Smith, Stephen Snoddy, Hannah Spooner, Angela Thirlwell, Julian Treuherz, Norma Watt, Jack Watson, Stephen Wildman, Neil Wilson, Christopher Wood and Suzanne Zack. The exhibition has been granted Government Indemnity under the scheme administered by the Museums and Galleries Commission, and we appreciate the role played by Gregory Eades in administering this.

I should like to express my gratitude to all my colleagues in the Galleries who have worked so hard to ensure the exhibition is a success. Sara Holdsworth and Howard Smith coordinated the exhibition administration and they were assisted by Kate Farmery, Ruth Greenbaum, Mary Griffiths and Tim Wilcox. Thanks are also due to Chrissie Morgan who designed the catalogue.

**Richard Gray**
**Director of Galleries and Museums**

# Introduction

Pre-Raphaelitism broke upon the British art world at the Royal Academy exhibitions of 1849 and 1850. An avant-garde movement aiming to regenerate fine art, it soon became the most talked-about feature of contemporary culture, exciting both enthusiasm and hostility. From the "visionary vanities of half a dozen boys" - as the poet and painter Dante Gabriel Rossetti later described the original impulse behind the Pre-Raphaelite Brotherhood - it was promoted by critic John Ruskin to become a nation-wide influence available to artists over the next half-century.

Its main figures have been seen to be, firstly, Rossetti, William Holman Hunt and John Everett Millais. Their personal example spread the word amongst their acquaintances and their exhibition appearances attracted recruits from around the country, while Ruskin enthusiasts needed no further encouragement to join up. Thus Pre-Raphaelitism rapidly became an important ingredient in the work of artists such as Anna Mary Howitt, Barbara Leigh Smith (later Bodichon), Jane Benham (later Hay), Elizabeth Siddal, Joanna Boyce, Rosa Brett and Anna Blunden. The personal association constantly expanding the number of the style's adherents brought friends and relatives such as Julia Margaret Cameron, Rebecca Solomon, Emma Sandys and Maria Zambaco within Pre-Raphaelitism's orbit. In due course, the original Pre-Raphaelites' pupils and children joined the throng, adding such names as Lucy and Cathy Madox Brown and Marie Spartali (later Stillman) to the movement's roll-call. Taken at first to be a mere retinue, these accumulated followers of the original impulse soon helped Pre-Raphaelitism to a second wind.

The principal figure in the style's later development was and is considered to be Edward Burne-Jones, though his life-long colleague William Morris should not be forgotten. If it was through the former that Pre-Raphaelitism eventually achieved a distinctive and distinguished overlapping with its rivals Aestheticism and neo-Classicism, it was through the latter that the Arts and Crafts movement became so fruitfully entwined with Pre-Raphaelitism. Numerous younger admirers of the style such as Evelyn De Morgan, Kate Bunce, Eleanor Fortescue Brickdale and Marianne (Preindelsberger) Stokes ensured its continued vitality, variety and visibility within the range of artistic styles as the Victorian gave way to the Edwardian period. Ruskin, though consigned by many soi-disant progressives to the back room of British art by the 1880s, continued to promote Pre-Raphaelitism and inspire artists to its adoption. Christiana Herringham and Francesca Alexander were two such talented admirers.

Pre-Raphaelite art is distinguished throughout its existence by truth to both nature and feeling, both actuality and imagination. Its hallmarks are a liking for poetical subjects, a belief in history as a living text, a desire to render the specificities of the natural world as God's creation, and a determination to bring social concerns into contemporary art. Its means are vivid colour, close observation, iconoclastic composition and intense, individual expression. The term Pre-Raphaelitism, in invoking the perceived purity of early Renaissance art, symbolised the modern, earnest searching for pictorial truth, beauty and moral meaning that underpins both its content and its forms.

Some of the style's adherents were male, some female, though up until recently the women artists have been hidden from histories of Pre-Raphaelitism. In fact, as a movement and a style, Pre-Raphaelitism was comparatively welcoming to women, while not mitigating the disadvantages of access and esteem which they faced in the world of art, as in society as a whole. This book, like the exhibition it accompanies, brings together paintings, drawings, photographs and other works that women artists contributed to the Pre-Raphaelite impulse during its long life. They demonstrate both that Pre-Raphaelitism is a broader historical movement than has previously been recognised, and that women were active in all its phases. Not only active, moreover; women artists played a crucial role in shaping, defining, developing and perpetuating the movement over its half-century. Our contention is that their re-inclusion in Pre-Raphaelite history will re-define its scope, concerns and achievements, as well as restore a wealth of forgotten and neglected works to public attention. Half the picture does not give the whole view.

In the early 1850s, a trio of young women with views as visionary as those of the boys of the Brotherhood dreamt of establishing a female network of "Art-Sisters", for sharing ambitions, studios, travels and strategies for success. "What schemes of life have we not worked out whilst we have been together!" wrote Anna Mary Howitt in reference to herself, Jane Benham and Barbara Leigh Smith, as the "germ of a beautiful sisterhood in Art, of which we have all dreamed long, and by which association we might be enabled to do noble things". Though the association was never formalised, the "Art Sisterhood" of Pre-Raphaelitism that endured from 1850 to 1900 based on shared ideals and aspirations informs and animates this exhibition. The work it generated bears witness in ways that have been unduly overlooked to the vivid importance of Pre-Raphaelitism in nineteenth-century art and its continuing appeal in the media-saturated twentieth century.

# Women and Art 1850-1900

## Jan Marsh

The world of women and art was changing at mid-century. In 1861 a picture entitled *Women's Work: A Medley* was on view in London, with explanation. The four ages of man were in the centre, this began, all being "equally the objects of devotion from surrounding females." [fig. 1] But the forces of Progress have breached the ancient wall of Custom and Prejudice: other opportunities for womanhood are opening. Doors are still barred by the guardians of Law and Theology, while Medicine laughs at women's impotent efforts to gain access to its portals. But in art progress has commenced. As advance guard, French painter Rosa Bonheur "has attained the top of the wall (upon which the rank weeds of Misrepresentation and Ridicule flourish); others are following. The blossom of the 'forbidden fruit' appears in the distance."[1]

**Fig. 1**
Florence Claxton, *Women's Work: A Medley*, photograph courtesy of Sotheby's

This contemporary satire by Florence Claxton depicts the situation of women aspiring to enter the profession. They faced many obstacles, external and internal, as well as vigorous competition from male artists in a keenly contested market. Nevertheless, many succeeded. As George Eliot heard veteran landscapist David Roberts observe in 1859, "If ever one sees a fine picture now, it is by a woman."[2]

**Fig. 2**
Barbara Bodichon, *Ye Newe Generation*, c.1853-4, courtesy of the Mistress and Fellows of Girton College, Cambridge

Our study of women working within the Pre-Raphaelite tradition during the nineteenth century illustrates the range and richness of their pictures, whose social and ideological context is explored in the present essay. Works of art come from complex interaction within the field of cultural production of matters public, personal, practical and conceptual. Alongside talent and inspiration, class, gender, opportunity, prevailing taste and change over time play their parts. During the working lifetimes of our artists, British society saw changes in both the professional world of art production and the experience of women.

Like *Women's Work*, the cartoon sketch by Barbara Bodichon showing "Ye Newe Generation" [fig. 2] reflects the sense of change and challenge around 1850. The following half-century was a key period in women's advancement, although in many ways the struggle against patriarchy still continues. Indeed, women's as yet unequal representation and prestige in the cultural field, manifested most visibly at national institutions like the Tate Gallery and Royal Academy, prompts the exhibition *Pre-Raphaelite Women Artists*, to bring into view work that has not been accorded due appraisal.

Middle class Victorian Britain - from whose ranks virtually all female artists were drawn - held female dependency to be normative. Women with careers were unusual and pioneering. For those like Howitt, Jane Benham, Joanna Boyce, Rosa Brett, Rebecca Solomon, growing up in the decade of Queen Victoria's accession, with its symbolic yet also meaningful elevation of a young woman as head of state, father was "head of the household", mother "the angel of the house". Sons were privileged over daughters, trained for careers in church, army or business, while girls were only to be wives and mothers. If they did not marry, women remained "daughters at home" or maiden aunts.

The population rose from 9 million in 1800 to 18m by 1850 and 26m by 1880, and the middle classes to around 25 per cent of the whole.[3] Economic growth through industrial production and global trade meant a rising standard of living for many. But when national statistics revealed a "gender gap" suggesting that one in eight women would never marry for lack of partners, the issue was of concern to a society where "ladies" did not work. At mid-century the first serious girls' schools were founded, so that education might emancipate middle class women from what Harriet Taylor in 1848 called "their present degraded slavery to the necessity of marriage."[4] Though not all benefited, women born in the 1840s and 50s like Lucy and Cathy Madox Brown, Marie Spartali and Maria Zambaco, Evelyn De Morgan or Christiana Herringham had opportunities unknown to their grandmothers and aunts, and by the 1880s and 90s girls also had access to higher education. "To an ordinary observer it can hardly be said that a woman's position is a hard one," wrote Mary Jeune optimistically in 1893, "for in the most important matters affecting education, training and choice of professions, a woman's field of choice is hardly less limited than that of a man."[5] However, numbers remained low and occupations gender-based. Much work was voluntary, which might offer an independent life but was usually subordinate to family duties. Marriage remained the life work of most women.

The struggle for art training followed a similar pattern. Less disadvantaged in some ways, since drawing and sketching were popular female accomplishments, young women with pictorial talents began, like young men, with lessons from a drawing teacher. Men then progressed, via private art schools, to free tuition at the Royal Academy schools, the recognised training-ground. Women were not admitted, so continued with private tuition, foreign study, or ladies' classes in government-funded art schools, including the Female School of Art in London.

cat.20
Elizabeth Siddal, *Pippa Passes*, 1854, The Visitors of the Ashmolean Museum, Oxford

cat.21
Elizabeth Siddal, *Lovers Listening to Music*, 1854, The Visitors of the Ashmolean Museum, Oxford

Family support was normally essential, though Anna Blunden made her way virtually unaided, and Elizabeth Siddal entered the art world as a model, before becoming Rossetti's pupil. Her training is visible in the early works *Pippa Passes* and *Lovers Listening to Music* [cats. 20 and 21], while the size

**cat 24**
Elizabeth Siddal,
*The Ladies' Lament from the Ballad of Sir Patrick Spens* 1856,
Tate Gallery

**cat 26**
Elizabeth Siddal,
*Lady Affixing a Pennant to a Knight's Spear*
c.1858/9, Tate Gallery

of *The Ladies' Lament* and *Lady affixing a Pennant* [cats. 24 and 26] testifies to limited resources. At the other end of the social scale, Spartali and De Morgan faced obstruction from wealthy families. "It may amuse you to learn that, when a girl, my sister was forbidden to paint, it was considered a grievous waste of time and unladylike," recalled De Morgan's sister.[6]

Many women artists came from artists' families, where instruction, studio space and materials were already to hand. Solomon, Emma Sandys and Lucy and Cathy Madox Brown trained at home in this way. Boyce and Brett had artist brothers. Later in the century, Herringham, Kate Bunce and Eleanor Brickdale came from families where menfolk were both wealthy and supportive.

From studenthood, men typically progressed through awards, exhibition, sales and membership of professional bodies. The pinnacle was election to the Royal Academy itself, limited to 40 members, all male. The irony that Angelica Kauffmann and Mary Moser had been founder-members of the RA was not lost on aspiring women a century later. In 1859, a petition signed by 38 women including Blunden, Solomon and Bodichon, appealed for the Schools to be open to all. The general advance of education and liberal opinion had produced a great change in women's position, this argued, so that "no less than one hundred and twenty ladies have exhibited their works in the Royal Academy alone during the last three years, and the profession must be considered as fairly open to women." The RA should therefore admit properly qualified female students.[7]

The following year, Laura Herford placed initials only on her candidate drawings and claimed the place offered. A small quota were then admitted annually, although exclusion from life study until the 1890s ensured that their presence remained separate and unequal. The growing number of aspirants is suggested by census figures; women identified as professional artists rose from 548 in 1852 to over 1000 in 1871. Of our artists, only Brickdale trained at the RA. Spartali was taught alongside Ford Madox Brown's children. "I shall never forget the happy working days in Fitzroy Square and the encouragement you gave us all to attempt to overcome difficulties," she wrote later.[8] De Morgan attended the Slade School of Art, founded in 1871, while Bunce received sound training at Birmingham School of Art, as from the 1880s the regional art schools expanded and improved under local patronage - from which Bunce also benefited in respect of works like *Melody* and *The Minstrel*

**Cat 48**
Marie Spartali Stillman
*Mariana* c.1867 - 9
Private Collection

**Cat 72**
Kate Bunce
*Melody (Musica)*  c.1895
Birmingham Museums and Art Gallery

**Cat 70**
Kate Bunce
*The Minstrel* 1890
Private Collection

**Cat 66**
Evelyn De Morgan
*Earthbound* 1897
De Morgan Foundation, London
(Bridgeman Art Library)

**Cat 65**
Evelyn De Morgan
*Study for Earthbound* c.1897
De Morgan Foundation, London
(Bridgeman Art Library)

**Cat 83**
Eleanor Fortescue Brickdale
*The Uninvited Guest* 1906
Private Collection
(photograph courtesy of Sotheby's)

**Cat 64**
Evelyn De Morgan
*Flora* 1894
De Morgan Foundation, London
(Bridgeman Art Library)

[cats.72 and 70, pp. 14 & 15]. At the same time, however, it was widely assumed that female students would soon marry, and that the decorative arts were their proper province. Many talented women were thus directed towards embroidery and illustration rather than the oil and marble to which they aspired, just as their predecessors devoted their creativity to copying and cross-stitch. By 1900, access to rigorous, inspirational, professional training still required determination as well as ability.

Access to the life class was a key issue. The Slade's principal in his first address noted "the difficulty which has always stood in the way of female students acquiring that thorough knowledge of the figure which is essential to the production of work of a high class."[9] Prevailing proprieties prevented women tackling figure work with the assurance of men, hence the timidity of their renditions. De Morgan's *Earthbound* [cat. 66, p.16] or Brickdale's *The Uninvited Guest* [cat. 83, p.17] display greater confidence, gained from the availability of the nude model - albeit "half-draped" or heavily wrapped round the middle - to women students at the Slade from 1871, and at the RA by the end of the century.

Life drawing also affected women's choice of subjects. As feminist art historians have shown, women traditionally entered a world where their own images served as signifiers of beauty, holiness, pathos or domestic virtue - a restricted range if masculine imagery is pronounced off-limits, and further restricted by inhibitions on women in regard to the visual expression of sexuality - the other great staple of art. Creative women had thus to produce art against an already determined background, with many of the tools withheld. Even when the campaign for life study was conceded, depictions of the nude by women provoked censure and derision.[10]

Travel was an element of further training, to study the masterpieces and historic sites of Europe. Male artists frequently travelled alone, with sketchbook and colour-box, or rented studios in Paris or Rome. Women seldom had such freedom. Meeting Harriet Hosmer in Rome in 1854, Elizabeth Barrett Browning marvelled at the American sculptor's independence, "She lives all alone (at 22); dines and breakfasts at cafés precisely as a young man would; works from six o'clock in the morning till night, as a great artist must," she wrote, noting also that Hosmer's emancipated lifestyle was free of all suspicion of immorality.[11]

A rough survey of British women artists suggests that they too were adventurous travellers. Of first generation Pre-Raphaelites, it was Jane Benham, Howitt and Boyce who most energetically studied outside Britain, not John Millais, Dante Gabriel Rossetti or Arthur Hughes. Julia Margaret Cameron, De Morgan (see for example *Flora* [cat.64, p.18]), Zambaco and Herringham also spent extended periods abroad. *England and Italy* [cat.13, p.67] shows Benham Hay's commitment to her adopted country, while *How the Virgin Mary Came to Brother Conrad of Offida and Laid her Son in his Arms* and *Dante at Verona* [cats. 53 and 51, p.21] reflect Spartali's domicile in Italy. Marianne Preindelsberger Stokes, who came to Britain on marriage, is a striking example of the cosmopolitan artist at home throughout Europe, an increasingly familiar figure.

Brett's restricted geographical range is evident in her Kentish subjects [cats. 6 - 8, pp.22 & 24 ] though Blunden's landscapes show she travelled widely in England and Ireland for the sake of eligible scenes such as *View near the Lizard: Polpeor Beach* [cat.12, p.23]. Lone women sketching were liable to be harassed or openly insulted, while practicalities compounded propriety when cumbersome equipment had to be transported. Howitt wrote amusingly of struggling up a picturesque ravine with easel and canvas strapped to her back, looking like a "very small Samson carrying off the gates of Gaza."[12] D.G. Rossetti wrote admiringly of Bodichon, who thought "nothing of climbing up a mountain in breeches or wading through a stream in none, in the sacred name of pigment". She was, he added, "quite a *jolly fellow*" in this regard.[13] Voluminous skirts and tight corsets were obstacles to sustained work. Rosa Bonheur's celebrated adoption of the workman's *blouse* provoked criticism. According to one observer, with her short hair Bonheur was "indeed not very distinct in the matter of sex as far as dress and appearance were concerned."[14] Few women wishing to practise art were ready to forgo their femininity in this way.


All however had to grapple with such imposed and internalized social attitudes. Throughout the half-century, gender prescriptions were vigorously contested. The emergent women's movement of the 1850s, opening up education and employment, paved the way for advancement but not equality, still less for the erasure of gender difference as the basis of social organisation. Male supremacy was regarded as God-given. The most women should seek was a separate sphere, not equal rights.

To many, this was unjust and socially damaging. From around 1865 when the first petition for women's suffrage was organised - by Bodichon among others - a steady debate grew over first principles. "Think what it is to be a boy, to grow up to manhood in the belief that without any merit or any exertion of his own ... by the mere fact of being born male he is by right superior to all and every one of an entire half of the human race," wrote John Stuart Mill (with acknowledged help from Harriet Taylor) in the aptly-named polemic *On the Subjection of Women* in 1869. He continued: "how early the notion of a boy's inherent superiority to a girl arises in his mind; how it grows with his youth and strengthens with his strength ... Is it imagined that all this does not pervert the whole manner of existence of the man both as an individual and a social being?"[15]

Given the conditions it was only surprising that men were not more arrogant, remarked Sarah Ellis, author of books on the Women of England.[16] From an early age daughters learnt to compete for paternal approval, to live vicariously through their brothers, to defer always to male opinion. Their duty was to serve and obey. "Some near relative may be ill, and a woman will give her care and thought where a man would not dream of so doing, where no one would expect it of him," wrote painter Anna Lea Merritt at the end of the century.[17] To be assertive, demanding, ambitious, was to be wilful, ungrateful and ultimately wicked. Already deficient in education, girls seldom challenged the parameters laid out for them. By the same token, small steps for men became huge strides when taken by women.

**Cat 53**
Marie Spartali Stillman
*How the Virgin Mary Came to Brother Conrad of Offida and Laid her Son in his Arms* 1892
Wightwick Manor, The Mander Collection (The National Trust)

**Cat 51**
Marie Spartali Stillman
*Dante at Verona* 1888
Private Collection

**Cat 6**
Rosa Brett
*From Bluebell Hill* 1851
Private Collection

**Cat 8**
Rosa Brett
*The Old House at Farleigh* 1862
Private Collection

**Cat 12**
Anna Blunden
*View near the Lizard: Polpeor Beach* 1862
Whitworth Art Gallery, University of Manchester

**Cat 3**
Barbara Bodichon
*At Ventnor, Isle of Wight* 1856
Private Collection

**Cat 7**
Rosa Brett
*In the Artist's Garden* 1859-60
David Dallas

In art, women's ambition was measured by the strength of their desire to enter the art world, men's by their aspirations within it, for critical acclaim and large sums of money. Women's targets were lower. *Nameless and Friendless* is the poignant title of Emily Mary Osborn's depiction of a woman artist before a supercilious dealer [fig.3]. Characteristic diffidence is illustrated in Louisa Lady

Waterford's request for tuition from D.G. Rossetti - her inferior in age and social status. Her studies, she wrote, needed "direction into a better channel than they are at present and are likely to remain for some time, in her ignorance of means to attain what she cannot but hope she may one day aspire to".[18]

Men's aspirations were further fuelled and women's aspirations dampened by the Romantic concept of genius that informed art through the industrial era. Strongly figured as masculine, the rhetoric of genius

**Fig. 3**
Emily Mary Osborn, *Nameless and Friendless*, 1857, private collection, photograph courtesy of Rupert Maas

**Fig.4**
Margaret Dicksee, '*Miss Angel': Angelica Kauffman, Introduced by Lady Wentworth, Visits Mr. Reynolds' Studio,* 1892, unlocated, photograph University of Canterbury, NZ

as a necessary element of greatness in High Art operated to exclude virtually all contributions by women. An outstandingly creative woman in European Romanticism like French writer George Sand was an anomaly that upheld the general rule. "The genius view of art acted as a deterrent to female ambition in the arts and in some ways caused a deterioration in the position of creative women," writes a recent commentator.[19] It set a "glass ceiling", if however high their aim they could never hope to reach the summit. Implicitly and explicitly, the highest female goal was to minister to male creativity.

In painting, images of genius beamed a "binary and biased" message of masculinity triumphant in William Dyce's *Titian's First Essay in Colour* (1857, Aberdeen Art Gallery), Eyre Crowe's *Reynolds' First Sketch* (1866, unlocated) or John Gilbert's *Rembrandt's Studio* (1867, York City Art Gallery). Even when Margaret Dicksee produced *Miss Angel* (1892), showing Angelica Kauffman visiting Reynolds' studio, it was no encounter between two painters of genius but "a frothy costume piece" in which Reynolds is the artist, Kauffman a deferential lady visitor [fig. 4].[20]

Some role models were available, however. Bonheur's landmark success influenced the rising aspirations of British women artists, especially after her visit to London in 1855 when she was, most exceptionally, fêted by the all-male Academy. Boyce's *Elgiva* [cat. 14, p.78] and Howitt's lost *Boadicea* of 1856 were arguably among the indirect results. In the 1870s, Elizabeth Thompson Butler's success, when *The Roll Call* (1873) entered the Royal Collection, offered new encouragement and stimulus.

With the women's movement's help, gender attitudes were modified. Ruskin's notorious view that "no woman could paint" (in the sense of painting great pictures) was contested by thoughtful men as well as women.[21] "I should like to see the question fully and intelligently discussed of what likelihood

**Fig. 5**
Kate Bunce,
*The Chance Meeting,*
1907, photograph
courtesy of Frost and
Reed

there is that women should compete in the fine arts with men," observed W.M. Rossetti in 1855, having Boyce, Howitt, Bodichon and Siddal in mind. "Talent and even genius is to be discerned among some ladies of the present generation." He hoped to see the issue fully revised. "A female Fra Angelico, for anything I can see, should surely not be a *lusus naturae* [freak of nature]."[22]

Of course, this was an "appropriate" example; a female Michelangelo or Rubens was evidently not envisaged or desired. And although Rossetti outlived the century, he saw only gradual change in attitude. George Moore's 1893 essay *Sex in Art* was echoed by W.S. Sparrow in 1901 when he complained that women of talent wasted their youth trying to paint like men, since female genius would never produce "its own Phidias, nor a Donna Raphael." If they must paint, it should be in a soft "womanly" manner.[23]

This was a rearguard action, but gendered notions continued to shape women's prospects. Art's association with elegant accomplishments meant that the boundary between pastime and profession was hard to police, camouflaging overt challenges to male supremacy and encouraging some whom the claims of high art would have scared. But it also promoted low aspirations and the snare of amateur status. Among our artists, both Francesca Alexander and Christiana Herringham chose to work outside the professional field, the elaborate *Roadside Songs* [cat.59, p.28] and the large woodland flower pieces [cats.77-79, p.92] being produced for private satisfaction. Spartali by contrast struggled to avoid amateur status. When she secured her first sale, her father urged it be offered as a gift. De Morgan's various works with female subjects seem to reflect her respect for hard-won autonomy.

Gender attitudes also governed media and genres. Oil painting had the highest status, so women tended to work in watercolour, chalks or pencil, making a virtue out of delicate drawing like Spartali or Alexander. Hence the preponderance of their works in these media. But *England and Italy*, or Boyce's study of *Mrs Eaton* (cat.16, p.31) and her unfinished *Gretchen* [cat.19, p.29] indicate ambition in action, as also do Lucy Madox Brown's *Margaret Roper* and *Ferdinand and Miranda* [cats.43 and 41, pp. 81 & 83] or Sandys' *Elaine* and *Lady in a Yellow Dress* [cats.28 and 30, pp. 79 & 76] when seen alongside drawings by the same artists.

Photography, the innovative art form practised by Cameron, was especially challenging, with its awkward equipment and dangerous chemicals. In choosing a highly pictorial style, moreover, Cameron registered a distinctive gender statement, only partly modified by the mimetic qualities ascribed to photography, held to suit women's capacities, and by her traditionally deferential attitude to her male sitters in particular, chosen as examples of creative genius.

26

In terms of genre, copying was lowest in the hierarchy of fine art, which moved upwards with still life and flower painting, portraiture and landscape, towards figure painting and sculpture. History painting was the most heroic. Women were held to lack "invention" or conceptual ability, and tended to carve out successful niches in "lesser" fields. Herringham began her career as a copyist. Sandys made successful portraits of children [cat.32, p.100]. Blunden and Brett came to specialise in landscape. Lucy Madox Brown's *Margaret Roper* [cat.43] or De Morgan's great allegories, or Bunce's *The Standard Bearer* [cat.71, p.34 ] and *The Chance Meeting* [fig.5] are evidence of other aspirations, however.

Size, too, could be a gendered issue. Just as socially women were instructed to be modest - the admonition "stop making an exhibition of yourself!" has an ironic edge in relation to women and art - so large pictures were seen as unladylike. Patrons might dislike ambitious work from a woman, paradoxically admiring exactly this quality in a man, so practical, ideological and commercial reasons combined to make women work on a small scale. Again, however, the size of Benham Hay's five-metre-wide *The Burning of the Vanities* (1867) [fig.6], De Morgan's *Dawn* [cat.61, p.87] or Brickdale's *The Pale Complexion of True Love* shows significant confidence. Bunce worked on a monumental scale with church paintings, while Herringham's flower pieces show that even within the private sphere she too desired "a large canvas".

**Fig. 6**
Jane Benham Hay, *The Burning of the Vanities* (also known as *The Florentine Procession)*, 1867, Homerton College, Cambridge

Marriage sharpened the practical issues for women artists. Throughout the Victorian age, men and women approached matrimony from different positions, irrespective of personal views. For men in professional classes, marriage meant financial responsibility in exchange for emotional and domestic support, and sexual pleasure. Women, by contrast, saw love as the paramount destiny and desire, displacing all others. Within the female sphere of value, a good marriage was as important as professional success was to men. "Women are so schooled about catching husbands, that the simplest species of civility from a man is converted into particular attention," while men feared inquiries as to their intentions, commented a writer in the 1840s, and with the mid-century gender gap men came to regard themselves as prizes and women almost as predators.[24] All were cautioned against marriage without a secure income, exacerbating women's fear of being left on the shelf. Spinsterhood was dreaded despite many satisfactory single lives and much evidence of marital misery.

Blunden's misapprehension that John Ruskin's friendly letters were a prelude to marriage is a pertinent example of courtship problems, as is Siddal's long engagement to Rossetti with its repeatedly deferred promises. Boyce, on the other hand, seems rather to have made her suitor wait until she was ready.

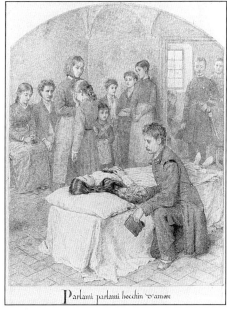

**Cat 59 (a), (b),**
Francesca Alexander
*Tuscan Songs* 1868-82
Ruskin Collection of the Guild of St.George, Sheffield

**Cat 59 (c), and (d)**
Francesca Alexander
*Tuscan Songs* 1868-82
Ruskin Collection of the Guild of St.George, Sheffield
Birmingham Museums and Art Gallery

**Cat 19**
Joanna Boyce
*Gretchen* 1861 (unfinished)
Tate Gallery

**Cat 68**
Evelyn De Morgan
*Portrait of Jane Morris* (study for *The Hourglass*) c.1904
De Morgan Foundation, London
(Bridgeman Art Library)

**Cat 16**
Joanna Boyce
*Head of Mrs Eaton*  1861
Yale Center for British Art, Paul Mellon Fund

**Cat 39**
Julia Margaret Cameron
*Zuleika* c.1864-7
Wellcome Institute Library, London

**Cat 38**
Julia Margaret Cameron
*Hypatia* 1868
Private Collection

**Cat 71**
Kate Bunce
*The Standard Bearer*  1894
Private Collection

**Cat 80**
Eleanor Fortescue Brickdale
*The Pale Complexion of True Love*  1899
Private Collection (photograph courtesy of Christie's)

Brett seems never to have had an offer, perhaps too bound by family duties to appear eligible, while Solomon's Jewish faith and artistic lifestyle placed her in an uncommon position.

As the century progressed, social relations between the sexes became easier, to the disgust of conservatives like Eliza Lynn Linton, who in 1868 launched a polemic against the over-bold and under-domesticated "Girl of the Period".[25] Women of this era, like the Madox Brown sisters, Spartali, De Morgan and Herringham, were thus freer to make their preferences known and ignore issues of rank and wealth - as Lucy Brown's pictures of young lovers seem to reflect [cats. 40 & 41, pp.37 & 83]. Spartali however faced parental opposition when she elected to marry an impecunious widower with three children. Change proceeded slowly. "I believe we are touching on better days, when women will have a genuine normal life of their own to lead," Geraldine Jewsbury wrote hopefully to Jane Carlyle in 1849. "There perhaps will not be so many marriages, and women will be taught not to feel their destiny manqué if they remain single."[26] By the 1890s, men and women could mix and mingle, play tennis and share taxi cabs without marriage being imminently suspected, yet marriage remained the main goal of women's lives and girls were easily persuaded to forgo education in favour of husband-hunting. Only a few saw spinsterhood as the preferred option. Though we have insufficient information, Bunce and her sister Myra seem not to have actively sought marriage, while Brickdale's *The Pale Complexion of True Love* and *The Uninvited Guest* [cats. 80 & 83, pp.35,17] and the allegorical *Love and his Counterfeits* (RA 1904, Christie's 1996) suggests sardonic observation, if not personal experience, of turn-of-the-century courtship.

Wedlock itself held particular implications for art as a profession. "In my young days," wrote Henrietta Ward, "most people would have agreed that a wife and mother had no right to be a practitioner in paint." Moreover, she added, "I think in most households it would have been rendered impossible by the husband's and relations' combined antagonism to the idea." [27] By 1900, fewer were so utterly opposed, but most nevertheless held that her first duty was as wife and mother. Yet marriage itself had altered. Men like Ruskin, who married in 1848, believed a wife's role was to please her husband and obey his wishes.[28] Twenty years later "companionate marriage" was the new ideal. Husbands congratulated themselves on shared interests. Courting Spartali in 1870, William Stillman self-consciously proclaimed there was "nothing in the range of human interest like a husband and wife who grow together in intellectual sympathy and aspiration."[29]

More than other women, artists were understandably drawn to marriage partners in the same field. Both continued their careers when Boyce married fellow painter Henry Wells, when Evelyn Pickering married William De Morgan and Marianne Preindelsberger married Adrian Stokes. Outside this immediate circle, the "art marriages" of Henrietta and E.M. Ward or Henrietta Rae and Ernest Normand were well known. Where both partners were not painters, mutual sympathy was important. Spartali and the Madox Brown sisters all married men with active interest in the fine arts. The use of husbands as models, as in Lucy Madox Brown's *Ferdinand and Miranda* [cat.41, p.38] or as portrait sitters for De Morgan and Cathy Madox Brown [cats.63 and 46, p.38] is a pictorial record of such partnerships.

**Cat 40**
Lucy Madox Brown
*The Duet* 1870
Private Collection

**Cat 63**
Evelyn De Morgan,
*Portrait of William De Morgan* 1893,
De Morgan Foundation,
London

**Cat 46**
Catherine Madox Brown,
*Francis Hueffer, the Artist's Husband* 1873
Private Collection

In many cases, women's earnings from art were an important element here, particularly so in the cases of Boyce, De Morgan, Spartali and also Cameron, whose art was closely linked to household finances. "Mrs Cameron did what women still do when their husbands fail: she went out to work," writes Mike Weaver. "The idea of her as a wealthy amateur is nonsense."[30]

Yet examples of companionship serve to underline the essential inequality within marriage caused by married women's legal subjection to husbandly authority. In 1854, in her role as pioneer feminist, Bodichon drew up a concise publication entitled "A Brief Summary in Plain Language of the Most Important Laws of England Concerning Women," which paved the way for campaigns against domestic violence and male appropriation of wives' earnings, among other reforms. "The notion that a man's wife is his *property* is the fatal root of incalculable evil and misery," wrote activist Frances Power Cobbe in 1876.[31] Legal power shaped relationships even within affectionate homes. Cameron contrasted her "delight" in making new images, with her "duty" to obey, describing herself as "under a promise *to stop* Photography till I have recovered my outlay that is to say to take no *new* Pictures & limit myself to printing from the old & depending on their sale."[32] Despite Stillman's fine words, Spartali's correspondence suggests conflict between his desire that she cease painting and hers to continue, not least for financial reasons. "Of course I have not the slightest intention of giving up painting," she wrote on one occasion; "what I meant was that for a few weeks my husband wishes me to rest."[33] The conflict was visible when Stillman claimed she was "baby-nursing rather than painting", but others believed she was doing both. "I suspect [painting] goes on over the baby's head," wrote Rossetti, "for I don't think she'd stop for that."[34]

**Cat 45**
Catherine Madox Brown,
*Ford Madox Brown at the Easel* 1870,
Private Collection

**Cat 47**
Catherine Madox Brown,
*Elsie Martindale Hueffer* 1895
Private Collection

Custom decreed that wives should take their husband's name - a matter of some import in the world of art, where name and reputation were closely linked. Most willingly acquiesced. Boyce, for example, exhibited after marriage as Mrs H.T. Wells. Evelyn Pickering happily became De Morgan (perhaps because of her family's hostility to art). Yet there was "no law to oblige a woman to bear the name of her husband at all, and probably none to prevent keeping the old name," wrote Bodichon in 1858. "To me it is very useful, for I have earned a right to Barbara Smith." Her husband agreed, "and if we have a line of English descendants they will be Bodichon-Smiths."[35] Ironically, she is in fact known to posterity as Bodichon, though the topic brings into useful focus the difficulty for both women artists and their historians presented by name changes - a problem seldom encountered among male painters. Jane Benham, another example, added Hay to her name on marriage, but never extinguished Benham. We have therefore thought it correct to call her Benham Hay. Spartali became Stillman on marriage, but partly retained her own name, exhibiting both as Mrs M.S. Stillman and as Mrs Spartali Stillman. There is some logic to these choices, but no rules.

At its best marriage offered women mutual support and well valued security, though this must be weighed against daily duties. As Anna Merritt warned younger women, the "chief obstacle" to success was that they could never have a wife. "Just think what a wife does for an artist", she wrote, half jokingly, "darns the stockings; keeps his house; writes his letters; [pays] visits for his benefit; wards off intruders; is personally suggestive of beautiful pictures [and] always an encouraging and partial critic." A husband was useless in this regard: "he would never do any of these disagreeable things."[36]

Moreover, at no time did fathers share in childcare, and thus maternity marked out the greatest difference in women's position. At mid-century contraception was little used. Like the older Cameron, mother of six, a woman married in the 1850s would expect regular pregnancies. Benham Hay's first child was born nine months after her wedding. Boyce had three in four years and might have continued at the same rate had she not died of puerperal fever, the ever-present hazard. High maternal mortality meant that one in 200 women from the upper and middle classes died giving birth. Childbirth, indirectly, killed Siddal also, for it was almost certainly post-stillbirth depression that led to her death from an overdose in 1862.

From the 1860s preventive methods meant that family size began to drop conspicuously, though gender symmetry remained an ideal. Lucy Madox Brown gave birth four times in six years, but her sister Cathy achieved a neat balance of two boys and a girl over a decade, with none in the nine subsequent years of her husband's life. Spartali, who inherited three step-children, produced a daughter and two sons, while Herringham's two boys suggest an almost modern small family.

Though servants undertook some child care, parenthood absorbed infinitely more of mothers' than fathers' time and energy. Henrietta Ward recalled being lectured by the widow of an Academician, "who said I was very wrong not to make my child's clothes and give all my time to domestic matters, and that if I did my duty to my husband and home there would be no time left to paint."[37] And while the physical burdens of child-bearing diminished, modern historians argue that women's cultural duties greatly increased. "Mothers were not only expected to meet the bodily needs of each child but to set the emotional tone of family life," devoting themselves the welfare of the whole household, including relatives.[38] In middle life, Blunden married her sister's widower, at least partly because she was in any case expected to care for his existing children. To such responsibility, marriage added legal security and, as it happened, a child of her own. Two years after she began photography, Cameron wrote that while she was at the age of 50 "for the first time for 26 years left without a child under my roof," she was nevertheless helping nurse another relative through a near-fatal illness.[39] Spartali linked this issue directly to impeded art practice in observing that the longer she lived the greater she found "the difficulties in a woman's way of doing anything *well*: if she has others to look after and care for."[40] This underlines the achievement of both Boyce and, especially, Spartali herself in combining art and marriage in a long and productive career.

The importance of children in the lives of women artists is seen in Boyce's *Portrait of Sidney Wells* and *Bird of God*, Cameron's *Baby 'Pictet'* [cats. 15, 17, 34, p.61], Benham Hay's *England and Italy* [cat 13, p.67] or Spartali's many images of her daughter and step-daughters. Their perceived affinity is also reflected in Sandys' portraits [cat.32] as well as Stokes's celebrations of maternity, her *Madonna and Child* [cat.75, p.41] and tapestry *Ehret die Frauen* [cat.76, p.44].

Despite the smallness of our sample, it seems however hardly coincidental that of the artists represented here, half were childless, and of these Bodichon, De Morgan, Bunce, Stokes and Brickdale enjoyed the

**Cat 75**
Marianne Preindelsberger Stokes
*Madonna & Child*  c.1907/8
Courtesy of Wolverhampton Museum & Art Gallery

**Cat 50**
Marie Spartali Stillman
*Madonna Pietra degli Scrovigni* 1884
Board of Trustees of the National Museums & Galleries on Merseyside (Walker Art Gallery, Liverpool)

**Cat 55**
Marie Spartali Stillman
*A Florentine Lily*  c.1885-90
Private Collection

**Cat 76**
Marianne Preindelsberger Stokes
*Ehret die Frauen* 1912
Whitworth Gallery, University of Manchester

**Cat 42**
Lucy Madox Brown
*Mathilde Blind* 1872
Lent by the Principal and Fellows
of Newnham College, Cambridge

**Cat 44**
Lucy Madox Brown
*Portrait of André* c.1889
Private Collection

most productive careers. Yet Boyce, Benham Hay and Spartali combined maternity and art, while the unmarried Brett and Alexander had the most exiguous careers. The Madox Browns more or less relinquished art on marriage while Cameron, Zambaco and Herringham only began seriously in middle age. All one can say with certainty is that marriage and parenthood impinged differently on women's and men's lives. What discussion of Victorian male artists concerns the number of children fathered (or not) by Millais, Hunt, Leighton, Poynter, Frith & Co.?

In her now-lost sequence *Scenes from the Life of a Female Artist* in 1858, Florence Claxton wittily delineated "all the aspirations, difficulties, disappointments which lead in time to successes." On the studio shelf a plaster head winks at the artist, at work on a picture of the ascent to the Temple of Fame. It is rejected and she is then seen in comical despair gazing at an enormous R chalked on the back.[41] Of course, male artists had their failures too; what was significant was the growing number of women with the confidence to aim high. For the exhibition record testifies to steady advance. As early as 1861, the press was hailing a new era in respect of works by Benham, Boyce, Eliza Fox and the Mutrie sisters. "Time was when pictures like these from a woman's hand would have excited a furore of astonishment," wrote the *Times*. "Now [each] takes her rank unquestioned and is adjudged among the painters of the year without indulgence being asked or given to sex."[42]

More was required, however. At a certain stage in his career, a male artist would take pupils, cultivate critics, establish a position as a "leading artist of the day". His works were in the major exhibitions and noticed in the reviews. Despite disclaimers, self-promotion was a recognised part of the process. Typically, women undersold themselves. "I recognise as usual that I have chosen a subject too difficult for my limitations," wrote Spartali, "and yet it seems impossible to attempt only what one feels sure of, it is so much more interesting to soar above one's strength."[43] They even offered convincing reasons for their own failure, as when Louisa Waterford described herself as someone who would have been an artist had she been obliged to earn her living and work harder. Yet more of the truth surfaced a little later, when she lamented her need for notice. "Not a creature cares, or knows, or observes if I do a thing or not, and if it is done, it is passed over unseen," she wrote. "Not that praise signifies, but poor humanity needs encouragement."[44]

Growing up in an artistic household, from the first both Lucy and Cathy Madox Brown were encouraged to aim for exhibition success, while Cameron took this step almost immediately she mastered her art, entering a contract with Colnaghi's. Professional artists needed to be seen at good venues, "where they could set out their wares and hope for sales - or ... at least the publicity and sales that would gradually lead to future commissions and sales."[45] At mid-century, there were six principal exhibiting bodies in London : the Royal Academy, the British Institution, the Old and New Watercolour Societies, the Society of British Artists and the National Institution. All were "variously discriminatory towards women".[46] In addition, annual exhibitions in Manchester, Liverpool, Birmingham and Bristol offered a showcase for works, where attitudes seem to have been less prejudiced. Our artists did relatively well, especially at Liverpool, where Spartali sold *Madonna Pietra,* for example, and De Morgan sent *Dawn* [cat. 61, p.87]. Blunden and Bunce showed in Birmingham, and though details are scanty, Sandys evidently established something of a reputation in her home town of Norwich.

The premier show was the Royal Academy, where Members' works took priority while other works competed anonymously before a three-man jury. There is no way of telling what proportion of work submitted by women was successful, but evidence suggests that rejection was a common experience. "I have been ambitious and had a disappointment - refused at the RA - I sent a monster in oil", wrote Bodichon in 1862.[47] Though it is true that many male artists also suffered unfairly, especially at this period when jury decisions were widely criticised, women seem to have been more frequent victims. Spartali failed when seeking election to some as yet unidentified body, which was perhaps one of the exhibiting societies.[48]

As the season opened, artists invited friends to their studios, thereby gaining valuable pre-publicity. If an admired work was not at the RA, the art world was abuzz with protest. A woman without her own studio might show under the auspices of a colleague or mentor, as Spartali did with Brown. "Tomorrow night I take in the pictures," she told her daughter. "The President of the RA Sir Frederic Leighton came to see my pictures today. Many other artists have seen them at Mr Brown's studio and I have I believe sold the one with the two girls."[49]

From 1857, the Society of Female Artists offered women an exhibition space of their own. Though supported by Bodichon and her feminist colleagues, it unaccountably failed to provide a mutual support system and attracted neither the best known artists nor adequate criticism and patronage.[50] Later, new venues like the Dudley, Grosvenor and New Galleries increased available exhibition space without giving parity of access. De Morgan and Spartali were among ten women out of 64 artists invited to exhibit at the Grosvenor Gallery at its launch in 1877. Here De Morgan showed *By the Waters of Babylon* [cat.60, p.91] and *Medea* [cat.62, p.48] in a total of 20 works over eleven years, and Spartali 17 works in the same period, including *Madonna Pietra* [cat 50, p.42] and *The Childhood of St Cecily* [fig.7]. Other exhibitors included doyenne Margaret Gillies, Sophie Anderson, E.V. Boyle, Louise Jopling, Anna Merritt, Emily Osborn (whose 1884 exhibit was a portrait of Bodichon), Henrietta Rae, Louisa Waterford, sisters Ellen Gosse and Laura Alma-Tadema and sculptors Ella and Nelia Casella. Newly arrived in Britain, Marianne Stokes showed at the Grosvenor in 1889-90, signalling her already established status. Yet, though women were felt to be relatively well treated by the Grosvenor, analysis shows that, of more than a thousand artists over 14 years, three-quarters were male - more than at the RA - while women's works formed only 17% of the total, and hung in the less prestigious rooms.[51] After the Grosvenor's closure, the New Gallery offered a good venue, where De Morgan showed *Medea* and *The Hour Glass* [cats.62 & 69, pp.48 & 49] and Bunce's *The Keepsake* was chosen as Picture of the Year [cat.73, p.50].

**Fig. 7**
Marie Spartali Stillman,
*The Childhood of St. Cecily*,
1883, photograph courtesy
of Phillips Fine Art
Auctioneers

47

**Cat 62**
Evelyn De Morgan
*Medea* 1889
Williamson Art Galley & Museum, Birkenhead

**Cat 69**
Evelyn De Morgan
*The Hour Glass* 1905
De Morgan Foundation, London
(Bridgeman Art Library)

**Cat 73**
Kate Bunce
*The Keepsake* 1898-1901
Birmingham Museums and Art Gallery

Critically speaking, as Pamela Gerrish Nunn has shown elsewhere and discusses below, when noticed, women were patronised and appraised by virtue of sex rather than skill.[52] Most criticism was unashamedly essentialist, commending the qualities culturally ascribed to women: delicacy, feeling, sentiment. Vainly, women protested against such thinking, or worked on regardless, and though male writers like William Rossetti and Percy Bate were more open-minded, others like Shaw Sparrow remained proudly prejudiced. All too often, however, women's works were simply ignored by reviewers, which, as Christina Rossetti remarked of her own endeavours in literature, was even worse than being laughed at,[53] and has seriously impeded scholarship.

To avoid such a fate, male artists used familiar networking practices at all-male gatherings. They dined with dealers in Pall Mall or went shooting with rich clients. They joined clubs like the Garrick, where artists and journalists mingled, and formed their own like the Hogarth Club in 1858-60 or the later Burlington, where Rossetti, Burne-Jones, Fred Sandys and Whistler exchanged "latest intelligence" on art matters. They cultivated collectors and created coteries, promoting their own and others' works. Founded with the express purpose of bringing artists, critics and patrons together, the Hogarth ignored women, so that on regretting Boyce's death, Ruskin added "I did not know her much, but I always counted upon her as a friend I could make, if only I had time."[54] He might have made the time, but the remark speaks for itself.

To an extent, women had their own circles. Most notably, in the early 1850s, Howitt, Benham Hay and Bodichon saw themselves as "Art Sisters", extending mutual support towards Siddal also. In the late '60s, the Madox Browns and Spartali were good friends. Boyce, Cameron, De Morgan and Brickdale seem to have preferred male networking, perhaps correctly seeing it as more profitable. Brett, Solomon and Sandys were reliant on brothers. Ironically, in view of the disparity between his own reputation and that of most women within the Pre-Raphaelite orbit, Rossetti promoted female as well as male friends, persuading Ruskin to purchase Siddal's work, and in all likelihood suggesting he add a notice of Boyce's *Elgiva* to his *Academy Notes* of 1855, as he did with William Windus's *Burd Helen* in 1856. He also gave Sandys an introduction to some wealthy patrons.[55] As expected, Madox Brown was equally useful in establishing his daughters and assisting Spartali. Burne-Jones was sympathetic to Spartali and Zambaco (to whom he owed an emotional debt) though whether this translated into public support is unknown. Overall, however, such networking as women enjoyed was but a shadow of that available to men.

As a result, patrons seldom competed to buy women's pictures. Questions of merit were not involved, purchases being largely a matter of critical favour and financial investment. Dianne Macleod's survey of Victorian patrons reveals no major buyers of work by women; indeed, few buyers of women's work at all.[56] Nor were female patrons particularly eager to own women's work. Ellen Heaton ignored Ruskin's advice to purchase from Siddal. Of our artists, most are known to have sold to private collectors, however, and certainly towards the end of the century the situation improved, De Morgan, Stokes, Bunce and Brickdale being among the beneficiaries. Dealers, through whom men like

Rossetti, Holman Hunt, Alma Tadema and William Frith increasingly sold work, took little interest in women artists, despite the prominence given to Bonheur by Gambart. Cameron used Colnaghi's, however, and Brickdale built a successful relationship with the Dowdeswell Gallery, selling through regular themed exhibitions.

In terms of exposure, sales and status, Brickdale and Stokes may be considered the most successful of all Pre-Raphaelite women artists, if success is measured in accord with the dominant, male standard. Thanks to her background, Stokes's St Elizabeth [cat.74, p.88] was seen in Berlin and Vienna as well as London and Manchester. Brickdale was the first woman to be elected to the Society of Painters in Oil, and later in life received a prestigious commission for the BBC's Broadcasting House. Stokes won a gold medal at the 1893 Chicago World Fair and joined both the New English Art Club and the Society of Painters in Tempera, though more public honours eluded her.

These examples illustrate the very gradual ascension of women in the world of art, where gendered disparity in opportunity defined its dispositions, placing women always in the margins. Success and fame were hard to attain. With talent and industry, many men achieved enviable status and incomes, manifested in knighthoods and high life styles. As Julie Codell has noted of typical Victorian double-decker biographies, compiled by widows or sons, "[a]bove all, artists figured as models of success ... thematized in the texts and in the images of large studios and houses and in portraits or photos of prominent portrait subjects ... or of their wealthy patrons."[57] By and large women artists were not measured on such models. Hence the paucity of information on their lives and works, and the very real excitement that attends their rediscovery.

It is too late to assist any women artists of the nineteenth century in person by bringing their work to public attention. Nor can the prevailing conditions of past centuries be retrospectively reversed. Throughout the nineteenth century, women artists were differently and disadvantageously positioned in relation to all aspects of picture-making. Cultural practices, as many analyses have shown, placed women's art in a separate sphere, a convenient excuse for oblivion.[58] But just as it is important to see their work in perspective, it is equally necessary not to compound past obstacles by continuing prejudice and neglect.

Women artists, active in all phases of Pre-Raphaelitism, deserve recognition and appraisal, as well as integration in the rapidly developing canon of the movement, which to our thinking is long overdue. The major Pre-Raphaelite show at the Tate Gallery, in 1984, for example, pointedly refused to consider any women artists, apart from offering a token presence to Siddal, then known primarily as a model for keynote works on view. In view of the expansion of both scholarly and popular interest in women's art over the past two decades, it seems even more egregious that the 1996 Macmillan Dictionary of Art, which lays claim to objectivity and authority, should mention only De Morgan in its extensive entry on Pre-Raphaelitism. We should like to see such histories corrected.

# References

For full details of sources, see Bibliography, p.157

1  Institute of Fine Arts, 1861catalogue, exhibit no. 316.
2  19 August 1859, BRP Papers, Girton.
3  See Joan Perkin, *Victorian Women*, 1993, 5, for reference to this estimate by Bessie Parkes, friend and colleague of Bodichon and Howitt.
4  See Gillett, 1990, 140.
5  Mary Jeune, *Ladies at Work*, London, 1893, ii.
6  Russell-Cotes Gallery, Bournemouth.
7  *Athenaeum*, 30 April 1859, 581. We cannot easily account for the omission of a leading artist like Boyce unless she was recovering from the birth of a child.
8  V&A, Special Collections.
9  Quoted Nunn, 1987, 52. In 1861 Margaret Oliphant observed the problem in literature as well as art, writing, "Even George Eliot is feeble in her men, and I recognise the disadvantage under which we all work in this respect. Sometimes we don't know sufficiently to make the outline sharp and clear; sometimes we know well enough but dare not betray our knowledge ... the result is that men in a woman's book are always washed in, in secondary colours. The same want of anatomical knowledge and precision must, I imagine, preclude a woman from ever being a great painter", Margaret Oliphant, 177.
10 See Nunn, 1995, chapter 7.
11 Letters of Elizabeth Barrett Browning to Mary Russell Mitford, Armstrong Browning Library, 1983, iii, no. 492
12 A.M. Howitt, 'Unpainted Pictures No.II', *The Crayon*, iii (New York) 1856.
13 Doughty and Wahl, 131.
14 Margaret Oliphant, 37.
15 J.S. Mill, *On the Subjection of Women*, 1867.
16 Sarah Stickney Ellis, *The Wives of England*, 1843, 69.
17 Merritt, 1900, 463-4.
18 16 July 1855, Princeton.
19 Christine Battersby, *Gender and Genius*, 1989, 5.
20 On the Victorian iconology of genius, see Susan P. Casteras, 'Excluding women: The cult of the male genius' in Shires; 1992 and '"The Necessity of a Name": Portrayals and Betrayals of Victorian Women Artists', in Harrison and Taylor, 1992.
21 See Nunn, 1981/2, 8-13 and Marsh, 'Art, Ambition, Sisterhood', in Orr, 1995.
22 'Art News, July 1855', *The Crayon*, New York, August 1855, 118.
23 *Studio*, 1901, 34.
24 Ann Richelieu Lamb, 'Can Women Regenerate Society?' London, 1844, quoted Perkin, 1993, 55.
25 *Saturday Review*, 14 March 1868.
26 See Perkin, 1993, 153.
27 Quoted Nunn, 1986, 121.
28 Virginia Surtees, *Reflections of a Friendship*, 1979, 270.
29 Stillman MSS, Union College, Schenectady, USA.
30 Mike Weaver, *British Photography in the Nineteenth Century: the Fine Art Tradition*, 1989, 154.
31 'Wife Torture in England', *Contemporary Review*, April 1876, quoted Perkin 1993, 113.
32 23 January 1866, UT.
33 7 August n.y, V&A.
34 4 January 1880, UT.
35 Barbara Bodichon, *An American Diary 1857-8*, ed. J.W. Reed, 1972, 134.
36 Merritt, 1900, 484.
37 Quoted Nunn, 1985, 134.
38 John Gillis et al, *The European Experience of Declining Fertility*, 1992, 43.
39 23 January 1866, UT.
40 13 September ?1881, V&A.
41 *Englishwoman's Journal*, May 1858, 208.
42 *Times*, 13 May 1861.
43 31 January 1890, Fitzwilliam.
44 Letters of 1875 and 1879, quoted Nunn, 1987, 184-5.
45 Trevor Fawcett, *The Rise of English Provincial Art*, 1974, 3
46 Nunn, 1987, 85.
47 *Letters to William Allingham*, ed. H. Allingham and E.B. Williams, 1911, 75.
48 Undated letter to FMB, V&A.
49 Quoted courtesy Mr William Ritchie.
50 For SFA, see Nunn, 1987.
51 See Newall, 1995, 23-4, and Casteras and Denny, 1996.
52 Nunn, 1987, passim.
53 See Jan Marsh, *Christina Rossetti*, 1994, 281.
54 Cook & Wedderburn, xxxvi, 374.
55 To Maria Leathart, 23 October 1864, V&A.
56 *Art and the Victorian Middle Class*, CUP, 1996.
57 Julie F Codell, "The Public Image of the Victorian Artist", *Journal of Pre-Raphaelite Studies*, new series 5, 1996, 11.
58 See Bibliography for works by Chadwick, 1990, Cherry, 1995, Gillett, 1990 and Nunn, 1987 and 1996.

# A Pre-Raphaelite Sisterhood?

## Pamela Gerrish Nunn

Historians of Pre-Raphaelitism have always tended to champion one or other of the original Brotherhood, describing the movement in terms of leaders and followers. None of the protagonists in this Pre-Raphaelite drama, however, is traditionally a woman. The female element in such a tale of cultural cut-and-thrust has usually been confined to the models and muses of the marvellous boys, Dante Gabriel Rossetti, William Holman Hunt, John Everett Millais, Edward Burne-Jones, and the wives and daughters of the great men, Ford Madox Brown, John Ruskin, William Morris.[1] This has been despite, or perhaps because of, the centrality to Pre-Raphaelitism's image and reputation of Woman. Woman - the object, icon, motif and motive of whom and from whom Pre-Raphaelitism is said to have been made - has, perversely, masked the presence within the movement of women - active, executive autonomous subjects making Pre-Raphaelitism.

Enthusiasts and detractors, if alike in their masculinisation of Pre-Raphaelitism, have always had various views of its life span. The present exhibition's chronicle of the style is closest in its reach to the schema adopted by Percy Bate, Pre-Raphaelitism's first historian. In his 1899 history of the movement, under the heading 'Pre-Raphaelitism Today', he declared that the movement was still full of vigour since "the principles of Pre-Raphaelitism remain as essentially true as when first promulgated, and work equally good ought to be the result of an honest acceptance of them".[2] The present project is close to Bate in its defining respect too; where other historians of Pre-Raphaelitism have simply excluded female artists, Bate noted a number of female practitioners active at the time of writing. Many women were indeed drawn to Pre-Raphaelitism over the years, and this exhibition seeks to restore them to visibility, scrutinising their relationship to Pre-Raphaelitism and giving a glimpse of the uses they made of its potential, which were various, rich and often unexpected.

For the original Pre-Raphaelites, the regeneration of British art was to be attained through a return to artistic integrity, achieved through truth to materials, truth to knowledge and imagination, and that truth to individuality which is called originality. Looking back to the early Renaissance, in which they relished, in Hunt's words, "the naive traits of frank expression and unaffected grace", these young people aimed for an art abjuring the sophistication, the visual gratification and the virtuosity of Raphael (at that time the most venerated of Renaissance artists) and his British successors, from Reynolds to Wilkie.[3] In place of academic characteristics such as perspective and chiaroscuro, angular drawing and naive observation aspired to a purity of form independent of pictorial formulae. The goal

**Cat 1**
Barbara Bodichon
*Dreams of Escape: Ireland 1846,* c.1846
Whitworth Art Gallery, University of Manchester

**Cat 18**
Joanna Boyce
*Shanklin, Isle of Wight,* undated
Private Collection

was a realism which convinced by literal resemblance rather than pictorial convention, by scientific exactitude rather than sentimental formulae and by the recognition of individuality rather than the deployment of convention. As W.M. Rossetti recorded, the group's founding aims were, "1. To have genuine ideas to express; 2. to study Nature attentively, so as to know how to express them; 3. to sympathize with what is direct and serious and heartfelt in previous art, to the exclusion of what is conventional and self-parading and learned by rote; and 4., and most indispensable of all, to produce thoroughly good pictures and statues." [4]

Pre-Raphaelitism soon flowed from the hands of many more than the original seven Brothers, manifesting itself as pictures which, in vivid colour and intense detail, in studied naturalistic poses and gestures, exhibited a high-minded and yet happily mundane cast of subjects, rendered with honesty and plainness and often a wealth of morally resonant accessories. Sculptures were fewer and confined largely to portraiture, in which scrupulous observation and natural detail replaced style and flattery.

Although Pre-Raphaelitism occurs chronologically as an expression of the Realism that displaced Romanticism throughout mid-nineteenth-century Europe, its ideals and enthusiasms retained much of the Romantic spirit - what Andrea Rose has called "the two faces of Pre-Raphaelitism" - as seen in Barbara Bodichon's *Dreams of Escape: Ireland 1846* [cat.1, p.55]. [5] On the one hand, the Romantic element of Pre-Raphaelitism is what makes Pre-Raphaelite paintings so blatantly distinct from the Realism of William Frith or George Hicks, which achieved a much easier popularity with the Victorian public. On the other, the Realist element of Pre-Raphaelitism is what updates it compared with the effusions of John Linnell or John Martin, who represented a grand but florid past. Here was a new respect for landscape painting and portraiture, an invigorated religious art, a living history painting, and a modern literary pantheon to complement the established names of Shakespeare, Milton, Keats, Tennyson, Shelley and Browning.

Creative women needed this alternative. Anna Mary Howitt, writing to Bodichon just at the time of Pre-Raphaelitism's formulation about her recent attendance at a Royal Academy lecture, expresses vividly the exclusion that women such as they felt from the existing circles of influence. "[O]ne seemed stepping into a freer, larger and more earnest artistic world - a world, alas! which one's womanhood debars one from enjoying - Oh, I felt quite sick at heart - all one's attempts and struggle seemed so pitiful and vain - for the moment - it seemed as though after all the Royal Academy were greater and more to be desired than the Academy of Nature...". [6] The new school or "Academy of Nature" as Howitt put it would offer an accessible alternative to the established artistic realm which women were used to observing longingly from outside. The "Academy of Nature" challenged or simply rejected the criteria and premises which traditionally excluded the female artist. It didn't acquiesce, it aspired, and here was inspiration indeed. Within Pre-Raphaelitism, surely the female artist could try her hand without a Classical education, without a training in anatomy, without unlimited access to scenes of modern life? Within Pre-Raphaelitism, surely those things she was told were her own especial strengths and concerns - sentiment, a feeling for nature, piety, neatness - would be adequate equipment for the journey to the heights of Art?

"If you can, get a sight of the 'Germ', a small publication put forth by a set of crazy poetical young men in London, artists mostly, who call themselves the 'Pre-Raphaelian brethren' and seek in all things for the 'simplicity of nature'", wrote Bodichon's associate Bessie Parkes to a mutual friend in 1850.[7] Women such as these were obviously not considered by the Brothers as beyond the pale *qua* women, for the fifty seven "immortals" on their list of heroes included Joan of Arc and the poet Elizabeth Barrett Browning, the latter with one star.[8] Ruskin's amateur friends Eleanor Vere Boyle and her cousin Lady Waterford were both praised for their work in the movement's early discussions, while women who came within the Brothers' acquaintance - Howitt, Benham Hay, Bodichon, Boyce, Siddal - were considered by themselves and treated by their male friends as artist members of the circle. Howitt was among those invited to write for the Pre-Raphaelite Brotherhood's short-lived magazine *The Germ*, and later *The Crayon*, the platform offered by their American admirer William Stillman.[9]

It was Ruskin's writings and lectures which helped establish a vivid image of the new style as far afield as the USA. He had a vast readership inspired by the aim of forging a meaningful art for the modern age, which included many women. The telling amalgamation of vestiges of Romanticism with Realism was eloquently presented by Ruskin, whose support of Pre-Raphaelitism was crucial to the emergence of a movement based on this style. His enthusiasm for the art of Turner and his taste for the Gothic were keynotes in the elaboration of Pre-Raphaelitism, reflected in the privileged position occupied within it by landscape and in its enduring medievalism. Ruskin's importance on an individual level is shown by the example of John and Rosa Brett, two aspiring artists living at the beginning of the 1850s still under their parents' roof in the provinces and only dreaming of the great works that they might bring forth if their devotion to Ruskin's great idea of "going to nature in all singleness of heart" should come off. Rosa's vocation, her understanding of nature and her talent for its depiction, were evidently equal to John's when they started out, but only he was able to attract Ruskin's endorsement. It was thus as an established artist that John wrote to her in 1860 with a combination of encouragement and exasperation, "I will tell old White to come and see your Pic[ture], also every one else of consequence - I shall hardly have the face to ask JR to come again - I don't think he would".[10]

**cat. 9**
Rosa Brett,
*Bunny*, 1873
Private Collection

In the Pre-Raphaelite family, Ruskin was the paterfamilias. He was prey to the typically Victorian generalisations about women's incapacity, as Anna Blunden found to her cost when she solicited his advice, but in his writings the female artist could find fundamental comfort. Habitually characterised along with the whole of her sex as a natural imitator but a poor inventor, she learned from Ruskin that Pre-Raphaelitism was the vehicle for her vindication. Though declaring that invention was necessary for the production of great art, Ruskin allowed that those who lacked this quality were nevertheless important to art: "Generally speaking, therefore, the duty of every painter at present, who has not much invention, is to take subjects of which the portraiture will be precious in after times", he wrote in 1856, in the fourth volume of *Modern Painters;* "the artist [is] to consider himself [sic] only as a sensitive and skilful reflector, taking care that no false impression is conveyed by any error on his part which he might have avoided; so that it may be for ever afterwards in the power of all men to lean on his work with absolute trust, and to say: 'So it was: on such a day of June or July of such a year, such a place looked like this: those weeds were growing there, so tall and no taller; those stones were lying there, so many and no more; that tower so rose against the sky, and that shadow so slept upon the street.'"[11] As his admirer Pauline Trevelyan wrote to her friend Louisa Mackenzie in 1849, "Nobody succeeds perfectly at first. You must have patience and draw from nature as much as possible. Don't wait for grand subjects. Draw a stone or a plant, or a bunch of leaves if you can get nothing else".[12] On such grounds Brett and Blunden, and later Francesca Alexander and Christiana Herringham, founded their ambitions, confident that social immobility and domestic restriction need not paralyse their artistic hopes, for nature was as much to be found in a British garden as on a foreign mountain-top, and art could be made out of it as much by simple observation as by learned contrivance.

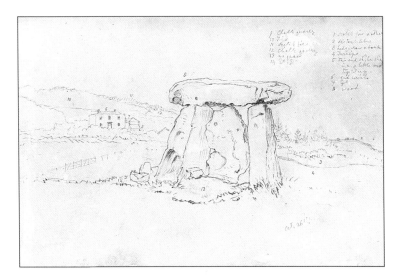

The fundamental principle of truth drawn directly from the study of nature was a recipe for those genres most readily allowed the female artist - still life, portraiture, "view-painting" - to be revitalised and a licence for the female gaze - previously expected to hover politely - to probe and search.[13] The paintings and drawings of Brett alone [cats. 6 -10] would provide sufficient evidence for the vigorous result of Ruskin's encouragement. Willing critics reflected Pre-Raphaelitism's capacity for acceptability *and* enterprise in the female artist in such comments as that which noted Blunden's *God's Gothic* (unlocated) at the 1859 Academy as " femininely gentle in treatment, yet powerfully truthful as regards the fact".[14] The same combination of qualities is confirmed by surviving works such as Boyce's *Sidney Wells* (1859) [cat. 15, p.61] and Julia Margaret Cameron's *Baby 'Pictet'* (1864) [cat. 34, p.61], in which a domestic subject is given searching treatment. Many more works that are presently untraced, such as Howitt's *Sensitive Plant* (1855) [fig.9], Blunden's *Foxgloves* (1858) and Brett's *The Hayloft* (1858) [fig.8] give vivid evidence of the enthusiasm and conviction with which Pre-Raphaelitism was seized upon in its first decade by the more adventurous female artists, keen to transcend that collection of clichés, maxims, beliefs, fears and prejudices called femininity which were supposed to define their capacities and efforts. Drawing their motifs from "woman's sphere", they nevertheless subjected them to unsentimental visual analysis. It is clear from journalistic comments that labelled Bodichon "the Rosa Bonheur of landscape painting" and Boyce "the Elizabeth Barrett Browning of painting" that the first female Pre-Raphaelites were seen as part of the "strong-minded" generation which formed the women's rights movement of the mid-century and made woman's role a talking-point in all classes.

In this light, it is relevant to note that no female Pre-Raphaelites were to be seen amongst the style's showing at the Exposition Universelle in Paris in 1855, nor in the Manchester Art Treasures exhibition in 1857, though Bodichon, Blunden and Siddal were amongst the Pre-Raphaelites in the exhibition of British art got up to tour the USA in 1857-8 [cats.11 and 25].[15] These seem to have been cases of

cat. 10 [b]
Rosa Brett,
*Sketchbook,* 1876-9,
National Maritime
Museum, Greenwich
**Fig. 8**
Rosa Brett, *The Hayloft,*
1858, unlocated,
photograph courtesy of
Courtauld Institute of Art

omission rather than exclusion, but the public effect was the same, to allow the male Pre-Raphaelites to seem the trend-setters and to make the women appear to be disciples rather than pivotal practitioners of the style. This distribution of credit, though natural to the conventional mind and welcome to the misogynistic one, short-circuited the fact that Pre-Raphaelitism was an art of collegiality and give-and-take, wherein women and men learned from each other.

But if Pre-Raphaelitism was essentially attractive to women, the intimidating effect on them of the style's early abusive reception and its continuing dismissal by some as ugly and morbid cannot be underestimated. Women's art was already the prime target of prejudiced criticism and trivialisation, and the earliest Pre-Raphaelite exhibits were dismissed by the *Times* as extravagances which disgraced the walls of the Academy and described by Charles Dickens to his readers as "mean, odious, repulsive and revolting".[16] Of their authors, the eminently respectable magazine the *Athenaeum* wrote: "Abruptness, singularity, uncouthness, are the counters with which they play for fame".[17] Individual works seen to be adopting the new style were variously reproached, patronised, tolerated and mocked. Howitt's *Margaret Returning from the Fountain* (unlocated), seen at the National Institution in 1854, suffered in this way. The *Athenaeum*, noting the "Pre-Raphaelite school to which Miss Howitt, perhaps unconsciously, inclines", reprimanded her for the vivid colour and meticulous detail which had become bywords for the style. "It is a pity that a picture of such deep and exquisite sentiment should be marred by a background of unmitigated green, with no tint gentler than that of duckweed or verdigris. Why should every leaf thus jostle with its neighbour to see which shall come nearest to the eye of the spectator? Why is each one veined and spotted with a painful labour and botanical research much misused?"[18] Of her Shelley subject, *The Sensitive Plant* [fig.9], exhibited the following year, the same newspaper claimed that "her delicacy of observation has grown almost

**Cat 17**
Joanna Boyce
*Bird of God* 1861
Private Collection

**Cat 34**
Julia Margaret Cameron
*Baby 'Pictet'* 1864
NMPFT/ Science and Society
Picture Library

**Cat 15**
Joanna Boyce
*Portrait of Sidney Wells* 1859
Tate Gallery

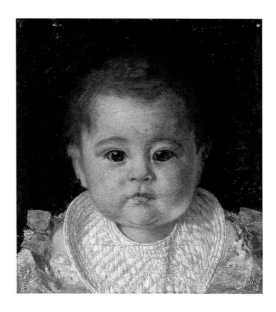

**Cat 4**
Barbara Bodichon
*Sisters Working in our Fields*  c.1858-60
John Crabbe

**Cat 11**
Anna Blunden
*'For only one short hour' (Song of the Shirt),* 1854
Yale Center for British Art, Paul Mellon Fund

**Cat 25**
Elizabeth Siddal
*Clerk Saunders* 1857
The Syndics of the Fitzwilliam Museum, Cambridge

morbid", and this exasperated observer, noting the "wearisome green salad of the background" and "mincemeat of raw leaves" of *Queen Boadicea* in 1856 (unlocated), declared: "This is Botany, not Art".[19]

This picture of an awkward, un-English, perverse art became in many minds the abiding image of first-wave Pre-Raphaelitism. Hence, though Blunden's *God's Gothic* was allegedly prized by its second owner, Sir Roderick Murchison, for its geological accuracy, the recurrent criticisms of landscapes such as *View Near the Lizard* (1862) [cat. 12, p.23] were that, though undeniably truthful, they were emphatically not beautiful.[20]

An extension of the controversies provoked by Pre-Raphaelitism with the potential to deter many women artists, hedged about as they were with society's demands for piety and virtue as well as artistic skill, was the moral question implied by the truth versus beauty issue.[21] In devoting itself simply to transcribing the material facts of the divine creation, Pre-Raphaelitism was in some minds skirting a form of heathenism. The female artist might understandably have preferred a safer stylistic path. "The motto of the pre-Raphaelites was truth, and in their pictures beauty was sacrificed to it ... Their works were all wanting in the highest grace of art - the ideal ... Put any pre-Raphaelite canvas beside works in which imagination and poetry have their true place, and the unartistic appearance of the former is at once observable - for all true art is beautiful and pleasing, not repelling and offensive", wrote one surveyor of the contemporary British art scene in retrospect, voicing the serious accusation that Pre-Raphaelites exhibited a fundamental lack of feeling and a basically mistaken purpose. [22] That this reaction lent itself especially readily to the dismissal of women's work in the minds of those who expected foolishness in a woman artist is shown in the case of Brett's painting *Thistles* (priv. coll.) at the 1861 Academy. "It might be difficult to get more interesting thistles", commented the *Art Journal*, "but they are only thistles after all".[23]

Female artists were expected, as members of their sex, to exhibit piety and sentiment rather than science and knowledge, to show an ability to generalise rather than a grasp of detail. The rejection risked by the female Pre-Raphaelite was, therefore, more complex than that which would hinder her male colleague in his avant-gardism. In this respect, it is unsurprising to find that those who most closely followed Pre-Raphaelitism's creed in its first period - Howitt, Blunden, Brett - gained little reward for this progressivism. The greater critical success of Boyce and Benham Hay, who did not so much take up Pre-Raphaelitism as take from it - in the words of one of Boyce's obituarists, "assimilating to [themselves] much that is best in the spirit ... borrowing nothing of the 'letter' as the common run of so-called pre-Raffaellites do"[24] - suggests that the thoughtful and seriously ambitious female artist did well to be wary of the style's intrinsic problems. She could perhaps operate more profitably for her reputation on its margins rather than at its centre.

In this light, it is telling that Boyce, though impressed by Howitt's spirit, claimed not to like very much her first success, *Margaret Returning from the Fountain,* over which all the card-carrying Pre-

Raphaelites raved. Boyce, in her female heads *Elgiva* (1855) [cat. 14, p.78] and *La Veneziana* (1861, destroyed), preferred to combine the fine handling, vivid colour and uncompromising observation of Pre-Raphaelitism with an appreciation of Venetian precedents, to achieve images of women that demanded attention even from Pre-Raphaelitism's opponents. In her turn, Benham Hay, though Howitt's companion in their formative years and fellow-student in Munich in 1850, produced a

homage to Fra Angelico in her 1861 Academy exhibit *Cloister of the Convent of San Domenico* (unlocated) which, in its moderation of Pre-Raphaelite handling with the post-Raphaelitism she had learned in Munich, Paris and Italy itself, struck Pre-Raphaelitism's antagonists and supporters alike as interesting and promising.

The potential problems of Pre-Raphaelitism for the female artist were most likely to surface in that topical subject Woman. The female artist who chose to include the representation of women in her work selected - perversely, it seems, for who could know better how to depict Woman than women themselves? - a particularly contentious site for her endeavours. Thus, it was not simply Howitt's Pre-Raphaelitism that critics demurred at but the feminism with which it allied itself, clear to see when applied to feminism's core concern, Woman. It may be in these terms that the contrasting absence of women from Benham Hay's paintings is to be explained. Her cast of male characters - *A Boy in Florentine Costume* (1859) [fig. 10]; *England and Italy,* (1859) [cat.13, p.67]; *Tobias Restoring the Eyesight of Tobit* (1861, unlocated); *The Reception of the Prodigal Son* (1862, Russell-Cotes Art Gallery, Bournemouth) - did not excite ideological opposition from her viewers but merely artistic criticism. Similarly, though Boyce touched upon the controversial nexus of women, sexuality and marriage in the abandoned woman and child of *No Joy the Blowing Season Brings* (1859, destroyed) - her equivalent to Howitt's *The Castaway* (1855, unlocated) - the range of female imagery within her oeuvre confounded categorisation as wholly radical. It embraced the demure (*Elgiva*) and the assertive (*La Veneziana*), the English (*Elgiva*; *Rowena* [1855-6] destroyed) and the foreign (*Mrs Eaton* [1861, cat.16, p.31]), the imaginary (*Gretchen* [1861, cat. 19, p.29]; *Bird of God* [1861, cat.17, p. 61]) and the mundane (*Peep-bo!* [1861] destroyed; *The Heather-gatherer* [1859, priv. coll.]).

Indeed, the responses to Pre-Raphaelitism presented by the work of these three talented, thoughtful, energetic women provoke the belief that, had Howitt continued her painting career beyond the setback created by Ruskin's dismissal of her *Boadicea*; had Boyce not met an untimely death at the age of only 31; and had Benham Hay become less alienated from Britain by her Italian exile; these three would have made a triumvirate to equal that of D.G. Rossetti, W.H. Hunt and J.E. Millais now routinely celebrated in the history of Pre-Raphaelitism.

**Cat 13**
Jane Benham Hay
*England and Italy* 1859
Dr Mark Hirsh and Mrs Jane C. Hirsh

Though Ruskin, considering Pre-Raphaelitism in his *Academy Notes* of 1856, declared "[T]he battle is completely and confessedly won... animosity has changed into emulation, astonishment into sympathy", it was a strategic overstatement.[25] As the next decade opened, Florence Claxton's determined and detailed satire of Pre-Raphaelitism, *The Choice of Paris* (1860) [fig.11] shown at the independent Portland Gallery, indicated how good a joke the style and its movement still seemed to some sectors of the gallery-going public, proving at one and the same time how familiar and yet how alien to the public its productions must have been.

THE CHOICE OF PARIS.
(A Idyll.)

Clearly, Claxton sensed that Pre-Raphaelitism was neither so passé that it was not worth making fun of, nor so generally approved that it could not be acceptably ridiculed.

The original and ultimate evangelist of Pre-Raphaelitism, W.M. Rossetti, wrote to the painter William Bell Scott about the following year's Academy, where Scott appeared to critical abuse: "Praeraphaelitism seems to have done its work in making people study more fully and accurately and paint better; and now the second stage is rapidly coming on - of more masterliness, stronger style, more painterlike conception and energy".[26] Ruskin had always allowed that the truthfulness of the style had vied in some adherents with the traditional attractions of the imaginative, but his early observation that "[T]he various members of the school are not all equally severe in carrying out its

principles, some of them trusting their memory or fancy very far; only all agreeing in the effort to make their memories so accurate as to seem like portraiture, and their fancy so probable as to seem like memory", came home to roost in the mid-1860s as Pre-Raphaelitism, beset by the feeling expressed widely in the art press that it had run its race, was confronted with the rise of Aestheticism and neo-Classicism.[27] By 1868, indeed, some declared Pre-Raphaelitism dead, that there was "only one eminent artist who remains true to his colours", and that the number of works by members of this school were "diminishing annually".[28] But the Ruskinian style was now established rather than extinct. As the *Art Journal* patronisingly complimented Blunden's landscapes at the 1867 Academy: "At one time it was feared that this artist was going the way of all PreRaphaelites. Mannerism, however, has been corrected in time, and now this little picture, which for harmony of colour is a perfect delight, shows the reward of faithful study".[29] In fact, Pre-Raphaelitism was at that point entering into a new and different phase, like a snake shedding its skin, developing a practice nudged into being by the challenges of nascent Aestheticism and reviving Classicism.

**Cat 36**
Julia Margaret Cameron
*William Michael Rossetti* 1865
National Portrait Gallery, London

**Cat 35**
Julia Margaret Cameron
*William Holman Hunt* 1864
NMPFT/Science and Society Picture Library

**Cat 37**
Julia Margaret Cameron
*Group from Browning's "Sordello"*  1867
NMPFT/Science and Society Picture Library

While the female heads and busts of Emma Sandys and her brother Fred - Tennysonian, Shakespearean and Arthurian figures of sorrow, longing and attraction - represent this move well enough, Cameron is nowadays the most conspicuous case of the "second-wave" Pre-Raphaelite. Her acquaintance with the originals such as William Holman Hunt and Thomas Woolner [cat.35, p.70 and fig.12] overlapped fruitfully and idiosyncratically with her enthusiasm for the essentially anti-Realist painter G.F. Watts and the errant Pre-Raphaelite Brother, D.G. Rossetti.

Cameron entered on the scene in the style's second decade to become without doubt the most celebrated Pre-Raphaelite photographer. The case against Pre-Raphaelitism, that it had confused art with science, was fuelled by the challenge which her chosen medium presented to painting. Professing only to copy the seen thing, photography led many art-lovers to hope that painting would put this upstart image-maker in its place precisely by asserting its own ability to do more than faithfully reproduce the physical appearance of the material world. It is from the battle between art and science that the work of Cameron, who began photographing in 1863, derives its enormous interest and significance. Her uniqueness is both impressive and disarming in its embracing and articulation of Pre-Raphaelitism's realism and romanticism in equal parts and follows on from the preferences of Siddal, whose output was terminated abruptly by her death in 1862. Both had a profound feeling for literary subject-matter, seeing images primarily in poetry, and both favoured the medieval over the contemporary. Cameron's *Gretchen* [fig. 13] is a sympathetic echo of Siddal's *Lady Clare* [cat. 23, p.73]. Cameron's efforts to create a religious art - in her words, a sacred art - from the "mechanical" medium of photography seen to have been born of science, reflect the second wave's attempt to take the spirit of Pre-Raphaelitism on from its positivist foundations to a more conciliatory, less austere future which allowed beauty to be a good in itself. She tried to rebut the argument that photography was not capable of art by infusing it with the qualities and applying it to the concerns of the highest genres in painting. A figure composition such as *Group from Browning's "Sordello"* [cat.37, p. 72] aims at the level of history painting, whose moral paragons a costumed figure such as *Hypatia* [cat. 38, p.33] means to parallel.

**Fig. 12**
Julia Margaret Cameron,
*Thomas Woolner,* 1864-5,
Musée d'Orsay

**Fig.13**
Julia Margaret Cameron,
*Gretchen,* 1870, The
Royal Photographic
Society Picture Library

Cameron belonged to the class that did not expect its enthusiasms to earn it a living and, though she needed to sell her work, was often dismissed as an overly enthusiastic amateur. More central to the definition of public taste in the 1860s were artists such as Emma Sandys and Rebecca Solomon, professional or jobbing artists painting to earn a living and thus needing to move with the market. They were guided by what would sell, and, in reworking Pre-Raphaelitism with more glamour and less reportage, show what could be forged out of Pre-Raphaelitism's established appeal once the anti-Realism of both Aestheticism and neo-Classicism came on the scene. Though portraiture would always be the stand-by of such artists, male and female, and child

**Cat 23**
Elizabeth Siddal
*Lady Clare* 1857
Private Collection

**Cat 22**
Elizabeth Siddal
*Study for Lady Clare* c.1854-5
The Syndics of the Fitzwilliam Museum, Cambridge

**Cat 52**
Marie Spartali Stillman
*The Enchanted Garden of Messer Ansaldo*  1889
Pre-Raphaelite Inc. by courtesy of Julian Hartnoll

portraiture such as *Anna and Agnes Young* [cat.32, p.100] and *Lady Winifred Herbert* [fig. 14] would always be the female artist's especial bread and butter, both Sandys and Solomon used their acquaintance with the Pre-Raphaelite trend-setters, who included their own brothers, to keep abreast of what was fashionable in the more ambitious, and therefore lucrative, field of subject pictures. In *Lady in a Yellow Dress* [cat.30, p.76] and *The Wounded Dove* [cat.27, p.77] both artists show they are *au fait* with the influence both D.G. Rossetti and the American painter Whistler were having on the changing face of Pre-Raphaelitism by the mid-60s.

**Fig.14**
Emma Sandys,
*Lady Winifred Herbert*
1870, unlocated,
photograph courtesy
Leger Galleries, London

**Fig.15**
Anna Blunden,
*Uncle Tom's Cabin*,
1853, photograph
courtesy Sotheby's

A comparison between Boyce's *Elgiva* [cat.14, p. 78] and Sandys' *Elaine* [cat.28, p.79] shows how far the simplicity in early Pre-Raphaelitism's aesthetic had been embroidered by that time, and to what extent the stern governance of history had been eclipsed by the suggestive inspiration of literature.

Any retreat from its original Ruskinian rigour that might characterise the style's second phase, though often now accredited to Rossetti's aesthetic evolution and his accumulation of a coterie, has as much to do with Ruskin's lessened prominence and authority in the late 1860s and 70s. Further, Ford Madox Brown and William Morris were as formative of this second phase as was the relatively secluded and isolated Rossetti himself, whose influence has been much mythologised. It is in the shadow cast collectively by these mentors that the Pre-Raphaelite women of the 1870s - the Browns, say, or Marie Spartali - produced their work. The style had now been in existence long enough to acquire a literal second generation and William Michael Rossetti was confident enough in its intrinsic resilience to welcome in 1871 a new group of Pre-Raphaelites in the persons of Lucy, Cathy and Oliver Madox Brown and their friend Spartali.[30]  He saw them as carriers of the same banner.

These artists collectively shaped a Pre-Raphaelitism mark two. Theirs was a dreamier vision of the past and the present, less fraught with the moral problems that the 1850s had discerned in both history and society, with more inner and less outer nature, more legend and less fact, more decoration and less documentation. Pre-Raphaelitism's younger recruits introduced the idea that truth to nature could be equally well "the woodspurge by the forest's edge or one's own inner nature - one's imagination and feelings - sometimes as unnatural and unreal as the chimera of the ancients".[31]  The equivalent of Blunden's *Uncle Tom's Cabin* (1850s) [fig. 15] in this version of Pre-Raphaelitism was Lucy Madox Brown's *Margaret Roper*  (1872-3) [cat.43, p.81]. The style's literary sources remained

**Cat 30**
Emma Sandys
*Lady in a Yellow Dress* c.1870
Norfolk Museums Service (Norwich Castle Museum)

**Cat 27**
Rebecca Solomon
*The Wounded Dove* 1866
The University of Wales, Aberystwyth, College Collections

**Cat 14**
Joanna Boyce
*Elgiva* 1855
Private Collection

**Cat 28**
Emma Sandys
*Elaine* c.1862-5
The National Trust: Lanhydrock, Cornwall

constant - Shakespeare is still found in Sandys' *Viola* [cat.31, p.82] and Lucy Brown's *Ferdinand and Miranda* [cat.41, p.83], Browning in Cameron's *Group from Browning's "Sordello"* [cat.37, p.69]. However, modern life subjects were increasingly neglected, a shift in emphasis already hinted at in Sandys' *Preparing for the Ball* (1867) [cat.29, p.96], whose contemporaneity is so equivocal that it has been mistaken in recent times for a Lady of Shalott. Nature was revered less for the wonder of its material form and more for its capacity to bear spiritual or sentimental meaning and the Ruskinian detail derived from the faithful observation of God's creation was transmuted into the keenly felt intensity of imagined reality.

The highly individual works produced by these artists in the 1870s expose the confusion of elements available to an artist attempting to move on from Pre-Raphaelitism but not necessarily to abandon it. Lucy Brown's intriguing *The Duet* (1877) [cat.40, p. 37], while original, nevertheless betrays something of her father, of Rossetti, of Ruskin and of Whistler in a composition which also reveals the fundamental problem from which the female artist still routinely suffered, access to rigorous training that develops a confident sense of space and the ability to render movement within it. A comparison between Cathy Brown's portraits of her parents [cat. 45, p.39 & fig.16] also displays the unpredictability of the oeuvre that could result from this transitional phase, with the figure of Ford Madox Brown exhibiting an awkwardness quite absent from the quietly dignified command the artist has given her mother Emma. Indeed, the female Pre-Raphaelite, in this period in which other stylistic developments were seen to be setting the trend, had still to work hard to make her own mark. Sandys' output is so close to that of her brother as to have proved in many cases indistinguishable. Cameron, in thrall to the charisma of her heroes Watts and Tennyson, struggled to have her own vision acknowledged. Brown's daughters Lucy and Cathy, brought up at their father's right hand, learned his peculiarities when they learned his skills.

In the 1880s, the general opinion came to be that Edward Burne-Jones' developing style formed a bridge to the form of Pre-Raphaelitism which would see out the century. In 1877, Burne-Jones made an impact at the first Grosvenor Gallery exhibition which some critiques linked unhesitatingly with Pre-Raphaelitism. "Mr Edward Burne-Jones, a Pre-Raphaelite painter in excelsis", announced the *Illustrated London News*.[32] His work gave comfort to those younger artists reluctant to abjure wholly the riches of the Classical tradition, permitting them to draw on a broader range of the Pre-Raphaelite. The paintings of Evelyn De Morgan, soon said to be "one of the most faithful imitators of Mr Burne-Jones", were, for instance, linked by critics with Cimabue, Mantegna and Botticelli.[33] Burne-Jones was the first to exploit the fact that, for all the explicit, defiant planting of markers in their original name, Raphael (and Leonardo and Michelangelo) had also appeared in the Brothers' list of "immortals". Not all devotees of Pre-Raphaelitism were happy, however, at Burne-Jones' influence. Harry Quilter wrote of the "dead carcase" of Pre-Raphaelitism as a source of corruption to the art of the 1880s, perhaps

**Cat 43**
Lucy Madox Brown
*Margaret Roper Rescuing the Head of her Father*
*Sir Thomas More* 1873
Lent anonymously

**Cat 31**
Emma Sandys
*Viola* c.1870
Board of the Trustees of the National Museums & Galleries
on Merseyside (Walker Art Gallery, Liverpool)

**Cat 41**
Lucy Madox Brown
*Ferdinand and Miranda Playing Chess* 1871
Private Collection

**Cat 33**
Emma Sandys
*A Fashionable Lady*  1873
Private Collection

Cat 67
Evelyn de Morgan
(a) *Study for Attainment*
and
(b) *Study for St Christina Giving her Jewels to the Poor*
De Morgan Foundation, London

provoked like many by the style's identification with the elite Grosvenor Gallery which seemed to them an alien and affected playground of the idle rich.[34] The Grosvenor formed its exhibition by personal invitation from Lord and Lady Lindsay, the Gallery's instigators. This was certainly an elitist practice but it brought an array of female artists into unusual proximity with the most topical of their male contemporaries, whose limelight they forcefully shared. Pre-Raphaelitism was presented at the Grosvenor as companion to both Aestheticism and neo-Classicism, and it can be argued that the effect of the Grosvenor's favour was to push Pre-Raphaelitism further towards a compromise with both these styles and ever further away from the memory of its original form. In particular, the status Burne-Jones developed there as a modern master encouraged the, somewhat contrapuntal, enthusiasms for Botticelli and Michelangelo in the work of Spencer Stanhope, John M. Strudwick, John Waterhouse, De Morgan and Spartali alike. The Leonardesque landscape background of De Morgan's *Earthbound* [cat.66, p.16] and her love affair with anatomy and drapery [cat.67] are evidence enough of the liberating effect of Burne-Jones' ambivalence towards a strict definition of the Pre-Raphaelite.

Even more emphatically, Burne-Jones' example sealed the style's departure from contemporaneity, if only until the next generation when Eleanor Fortescue Brickdale and others re-established the habit of contemporary commentary through an historical vocabulary. Burne-Jones' much-repeated testament that "I mean by a picture a beautiful romantic dream of something that never was, never will be - in light better than any light that ever shone - in a land no-one can define, or remember, only desire"[35] encouraged Pre-Raphaelitism's withdrawal from reportage of the modern world into the expression of individual flights of fancy, still bearing moral and spiritual messages but in increasingly allusive and subjective language.[36] Certainly the still productive Brett, for instance, had she been brought to the Lindsays' notice, would not have fitted into their vision of contemporary art. It was, then, just as well for Pre-Raphaelitism's survival that its appeal remained broad, with many of its male practitioners still appearing at the Academy. Though neither De Morgan nor Spartali was seen there after 1877, they flew the flag at important regional exhibitions such as those in Liverpool and Birmingham, long provincial centres of Pre-Raphaelite enthusiasm.

Perhaps another element of "third-wave" Pre-Raphaelitism in Quilter's mind when he suggested its moral dubiousness was its use of the nude, a standard motif in the western tradition which had, however, been almost totally absent from Pre-Raphaelitism in its original form as a predominantly Realist art. Not only in Burne-Jones' work, but in that of all artists inspired by him, the naked body enjoyed a resurgence equal to that concurrently visible in the neo-Classicists. This apparent ubiquity of unclothed men and women in contemporary art gave rise in the mid 1880s to loud controversy, of which female artists were bound to be the particular victims, given the entanglement of the nude with sexual morality and social etiquette.[37] Though women of De Morgan's generation were able to study from life much more freely than any before them, internal inhibition and public disapproval could still hinder and enfeeble the art of older women working at this time. Hence the tentative handling of figures and the hesitant physical forms, even when clothed, of Spartali's compositions such as *How the Virgin Mary Came to Brother Conrad of Offida and Laid her Son in his Arms* [cat.53, p.21] and *Dante at Verona* [cat.51, p.21], which contrast significantly with the dynamism and conviction of the protagonists in De Morgan's *Dawn* [cat.61, p.87] and *Flora* [cat. 64, p.18]. It is not only Spartali's personal sensibility that informs her work with this Kauffmanesque ambivalence towards the human form, but also the vexed question of the female artist's relation to the body. The female artist was generally still likely to win greater approval for the decorative than the daring, though the upper-class De Morgan, less dependent on critical opinion than the majority of her contemporaries, seems to have consulted none but her own sensibility in her choice of motifs.

This controversy over the nude can be supposed, however, to have directed some female artists in the later 1880s and 1890s towards an overtly chaste, not to say, devotional art such as is seen towards the end of the century taking quite a hold on Spartali's output and dominating the work of Kate Bunce and Marianne Stokes. Spartali's attention to saints' stories (e.g. *How the Virgin Mary Came to Brother Conrad of Offida* [cat.53] and *St Cecily* [fig. 7, p.47]) is taken further in the younger Bunce's inclusion of devotional objects in *Melody* [cat.72, p.14], *The Keepsake* [cat.73, p.50] and *The Chance Meeting* [fig.5, p.26] and selection of Biblical subjects such as St John the Baptist (*Vox Clamantis in Deserto*, 1889, unlocated) and Jairus' daughter (*Talitha Cumi*, 1905, unlocated). Correspondingly, Stokes established religious subjects as one of her specialisms at both the Academy and the New Gallery between 1889 and 1907 with well-received canvases such as *Angels Entertaining the Holy Child* (1893, Pym's Gallery 1983) and *St Elizabeth of Hungary Spinning for the Poor* (1895) [cat.74, p.88]. The use of winged figures in both De Morgan's and Brickdale's work should perhaps be seen as a non-denominational equivalent of this trend away from material forms and towards a more spiritual vocabulary which no doubt reflects the anxiety provoked by the coming turn of the century.

**Cat 61**
Evelyn De Morgan
*Dawn (Aurora Triumphans)* 1886
Russell-Cotes Art Gallery and Museum, Bournemouth

**Cat 74**
Marianne Preindelsberger Stokes
*St Elizabeth of Hungary Spinning for the Poor* 1895
Private Collection (photograph courtesy of Magdalen Evans)

**Cat 54**
Marie Spartali Stillman
*St. George* 1892
Delaware Art Museum

As Allen Staley has pointed out, viewers of the 1886 Millais and Hunt exhibitions were able "to see for the first time how different the dazzling colours and scrupulous naturalism of early Pre-Raphaelite pictures were not only from Millais' mature style, but also from the later Pre-Raphaelitism which in the hands of Burne-Jones had evolved into the Aestheticism dominating the summer exhibitions of the Grosvenor Gallery".[38] When links were looked for that might explain the disparities between the current form of the style and its original, the female artist perversely came into her own, assumed as she still was to be a natural imitator. De Morgan, Spartali and, later, Bunce and Brickdale were frequently cited as confirmation of the survival of Pre-Raphaelitism on the ground that their work resembled or took from the earlier Pre-Raphaelites. "[A] Rossetti translated, if that were possible, by Mr. Ford Madox Brown", wrote F.G. Stephens of Spartali's work at the New Gallery in 1889.[39] Some observers such as he, clearly still unable or unwilling to allow that any of what the female artist achieved was to her own credit, cited these artists' perceived genealogy not as credit, however, but as debit. The observation provoked in 1893 by Spartali's work at the New Gallery that the tradition of Ford Madox Brown survived in the work of "one of the most intelligent, if most mannered, of his disciples" was a very mixed blessing.[40] The erstwhile Brother F.G. Stephens, art critic for the *Athenaeum* until 1901, constantly belittled women's contribution to this fin-de-siècle Pre-Raphaelitism by comparison with its heroes. Typical was the telling-off he gave Bunce's *The Day-dream* [fig. 17] at the 1892 Academy: "We fear Miss Bunce, who has respectable notions of painting, has mistaken her vocation in trying to follow Rossetti".[41]

Such appraisals, which distorted unconscionably the contribution women artists made in the 1890s to the survival of the style, ignore the individualism as well as degrading the fidelity of these artists' versions of Pre-Raphaelitism, which in this period were presented to the gallery-going public on a much larger, eye-catching scale than in previous generations. Stephens' and like assessments rejected completely both the dramatic imagination of De Morgan and the decorative sensibility of Bunce, as well as the quiet lyricism of Spartali and the narrative power of Brickdale. Such a view tried, even half a century after women had shown themselves to be a part of Pre-Raphaelitism, to deny both that women belonged in this radical, trend-setting movement, and, perhaps more crucially in the patriarchal mind, that it in some way belonged to them.

The coming of a new age which would see the eventual demise of Pre-Raphaelitism was presaged in the deaths in the century's last decade of some of the perceived leaders of the movement's long march. Brown died in 1893, Morris and Millais in 1896, Burne-Jones in 1898, and, most seismic of all, Ruskin in 1900. However, the enduring impression made on the face of British art by he whom many thought the architect of Pre-Raphaelitism is shown in the modest power of the work Alexander

**Cat 60**
Evelyn De Morgan
*By the Waters of Babylon* 1883
De Morgan Foundation, London
(Bridgeman Art Library)

**Cat 79 (b)**
Christiana Herringham
*Yellow Flags* c.1900-10
Lent by the Principal and Fellows of
Newnham College, Cambridge

**Cat 77**
Christiana Herringham
*Foxgloves & Brambles* c.1900-10
Lent by the Principal and Fellows of
Newnham College, Cambridge

**Cat 78**
Christiana Herringham
*Wild Clematis & Brambles* c.1900-10
Lent by the Principal and Fellows of
Newnham College, Cambridge

and Herringham [cats. 59, 77-79] made in Ruskin's twilight years. Retrospective exhibitions, catalogues raisonnés and double-volume biographies followed the spate of deaths, reasserting the dominance in Pre-Raphaelitism's long life of the male vision and voice. It is De Morgan and Brickdale, however, who show the most eloquent examples of a quiet determination to perpetuate as long as possible the great style of the nineteenth century, the former with her enigmatic parables such as *The Hour Glass* (1904)[cat. 69, p.49] and later works that encompass even the cataclysm of the First World War and the latter with her moral narratives from poetry, legend, fairy-tale and history such as *The Uninvited Guest* (1906) [cat. 83, p.17].

The persistent validity of Pre-Raphaelitism was asserted as well in the establishment in 1893 of *The Studio* magazine. This was a self-conscious attempt to keep its flame burning. It gave willing coverage to the current male and female Pre-Raphaelites, demonstrating incidentally what a fillip to the style's survival the Arts and Crafts Movement had been in the attention it paid to the Birmingham school to which the Bunce sisters belonged and the Glasgow school in which Charles Rennie Mackintosh, the MacDonald sisters, Jessie King, Jessie Newbery and Anne MacBeth were prominent. In 1898, *The Studio* ran an article couched in the form of a conversation among three observers of the British art scene. It took the state of Pre-Raphaelitism and its image as an important end-of-century question provoked by the occasion of the Royal Academy's Millais exhibition and the Rossetti exhibition at the New Gallery. The three agreed that there was still such a thing as Pre-Raphaelitism: "No matter what the Pre-Raphaelite Brotherhood actually meant, or what Mr Ruskin put forward as their creed, the movement we see developed today is deeper and broader than they guessed. It began before them, and it has lasted beyond them".[42]

**Cat 85**
Eleanor Fortescue
Brickdale
*Guinevere* 1911
Birmingham Museums
and Art Gallery

This was the spirit in which, in 1902, Marion Hepworth Dixon characterised Brickdale as almost the saviour of a proud tradition in danger of oblivion, citing Ford Madox Brown as her noble ancestor: "Not that the artist in question is an imitator or conscious follower of any master whatsoever", he wrote. "But...we deal with an artist who has drunk at wholesome and fortifying springs".[43] Indeed, the number of subjects taken by Brickdale already treated by earlier Pre-Raphaelite artists - *Guinevere* [cat. 85] is a case in point - signalled its enduring inspiration for her. She continued to represent Pre-Raphaelitism on its old battleground, the Academy, until 1922, attaining a popular visibility equal to that which the style had originally enjoyed. Her industry in watercolour, exemplified by *I did no more* (1908) [cat.84, p.95] and *Pride and Ambition* (1915) [cat.86, p.95], gave her not only a huge audience but a widespread influence over other artists working at the start of the new century with the remains of Pre-Raphaelitism, such as Margaret and Frances MacDonald.

**Cat 81**
Eleanor Fortescue Brickdale
*The Ugly Princess* c.1902
Private Collection

**Cat 84**
Eleanor Fortescue
Brickdale
*I did no more while my
heart was warm* 1908
The Visitors of the
Ashmolean Museum,
Oxford

**Cat 86**
Eleanor Fortescue
Brickdale
*Pride and Ambition here/
Only in far-fetched
metaphors appear* 1915
The Visitors of the
Ashmolean Museum,
Oxford

**Cat 29**
Emma Sandys
*Preparing for the Ball* 1867
Private Collection

**Cat 49**
Marie Spartali Stillman
*Self Portrait* 1871
Delaware Art Museum

As Andrea Rose has observed, the last Pre-Raphaelites testify to the fact that the first Pre-Raphaelites "left a legacy of thought that encourages artists to work in defiance of smugness and indifference, and often in revolt against popular expectations".[44] That legacy animated the varied work of De Morgan, Bunce, Brickdale and Stokes and others such as Maria Zambaco whose chief contribution is in the applied arts. Their work in all media displays the characteristics of vivid colour, attention to detail, medievalism, love of poetry and moral consciousness that can be expected from Pre-Raphaelitism at any stage in its long life. Some habits were clearly dear to every Pre-Raphaelite generation. The figure in nature seen in Howitt's *Sensitive Plant* [fig. 9, p.60] and Benham Hay's *England and Italy* [cat.13, p.67], Siddal's *The Ladies Lament* [cat.24, p.12] and Sandys' *Lady Winfred Herbert* [fig. 14, p.75], De Morgan's *Flora* [cat. 64, p.18] and Brickdale's *The Little Foot Page* [cat.82, frontispiece] is a fundamental expression of the style's belief in the affinity between humanity and the pure, truthful beauty of nature. Equally, Herringham's attempt, with Bunce, Stokes and others, to revive tempera as a painting medium displays the same earnest striving after the redemption of art that underpinned the earliest Pre-Raphaelite efforts. In her significant essay on the subject, prefacing the first exhibition of the Society of Painters in Tempera (1905), Herringham strikes the same note of idealism that resonated through the work of the 1850s: "[Oil] too readily lends itself to false finish and smugness", she declared, citing a familiar hero in Fra Angelico. Likewise, the note of piety struck in the works of Bunce [cat. 72] and Stokes [cats. 74, 76], the spiritual if not religious tenor of much of De Morgan's and Brickdale's early twentieth-century work, echoes the Christian Socialist aspect of the first Pre-Raphaelitism. The rich fabric which Pre-Raphaelitism had become by the dawn of the new century may have been the costume of a passing age, but its many layers gave it a resistance to the chilly winds of Modernism, allowing it not only to survive but to prosper until the war, which brought the death of so much.

In 1905, Hunt brought out his massive and would-be definitive testament, *Pre-Raphaelitism and the Pre-Raphaelite Brotherhood*. It gave little credit to the female artists who had helped make and prolong the style. Women's part in that process was, indeed, still questioned by many, but, as this exhibition testifies, they all produced work which adds an entire dimension to our understanding of Pre-Raphaelitism's rise, development and influence and whose neglect prevents a full assessment of this trend so significant in British art. This exhibition shows that these have been unjustly neglected artists, revealing that they, in the words of one of Spartali's obituarists, "had no little share in creating the influence which, half a century ago, the circle exercised over the whole art and life of that age".[45] This exhibition presumes that to know what women's Pre-Raphaelitism looked like, how it was received, and what it had to say, is necessary to the building of a more complete picture of this bright thread running through the sometimes dull fabric of nineteenth-century British art. It is carried out rather in the spirit expressed by one of De Morgan's obituarists, whose observation can be extended to all the artists represented here: "The present age is not in sympathy with symbolism and the things dealing with eternal truths. A future generation will doubtless turn to them again, and it is safe to prophesy that Evelyn De Morgan's works will be as eagerly sought after as some of the Old Masters are today".[46]

**Cat 56**
Maria Zambaco
*Young Girl* 1885
Permission of the Trustees of the
British Museum
(reverse *Anemones*)

**Cat 58**
Maria Zambaco
*Margherita di Prato* 1886
Permission of the Trustees of the
British Museum

**Cat 57**
Maria Zambaco
*Marie Stillman* 1886
Permission of the Trustees of the
British Museum
(reverse *Lily*)

99

**Cat 32**
Emma Sandys
*Anna and Agnes Young* 1870
Private Collection

# References

1 John Gere's show at the Whitechapel Gallery, 1972, included no female artists and the Tate Gallery's would-be definitive exhibition, 1984, had Elizabeth Siddal as a token woman among its 29 artists.
2 Bate, 1899, 117.
3 Hunt, 1905, i, 130-1.
4 Rossetti, 1895, i, 135.
5 Rose, 1981, 8.
6 Barbara Stephen notebook, Cambridge 7621/70.
7 Parkes Papers, Girton College.
8 See Hunt, 1905,i, 159 (Jesus being given four stars).
9 See Casteras, 1990.
10 Unpublished letter from John Brett to Rosa Brett, 22 March 1860 (artist's family).
11 *Modern Painters*, iv, ch. 2, Cook and Wedderburn, vi, 31
12 Quoted in Trevelyan, 1978, 47.
13 "Pre-Raphaelitism has but one principle", declared Ruskin in 1854, "that of absolute, uncompromising truth in all that it does, obtained by working everything down to the most minute detail, from nature and from nature only". (Lectures on Architecture and Painting: Pre-Raphaelitism (1854), Cook and Wedderburn, xii, 157).
14 *The Critic*, 21 May 1859, 497.
15 See Casteras, 1990, ch.3.
16 Dickens, 1850, 265.
17 The *Athenaeum*, 1 June 1850, 590.
18 Ibid., 19 March 1854, p.346.
19 Ibid., 21 March 1855, 351 and 7 June 1856, 718.
20 See Anonymous, 1898, 205-9.
21 See Catherine Barnes Stevenson, "How it struck a Contemporary", *The Victorian Newsletter*, Fall 1981, 8-14.
22 Anonymous, 1868, 312.
23 1 July 1861, 195.
24 *The Critic*, 27 July 1861, 110.
25 Academy Notes (1856), Cook and Wedderburn, xiv, 47
26 WM Rossetti to WB Scott, 8 May 1861, Peattie, 117.
27 Lectures on Painting and Architecture: Pre-Raphaelitism (1854), 157.
28 Anonymous, 1868, 312.  Hunt was the one practitioner meant.
29 1 June 1867, 145.
30 Rossetti, 1871, 47-9.
31 Rose, 9.
32 "The Grosvenor Gallery", 12 May 1877, 450.
33 *The Magazine of Art*, May 1881, 179.
34 Quilter, 1880, 395.
35 Quoted Arts Council 1975, 11.
36 Ruskin defended this apparent move away from the truthfulness he had praised in the Pre-Raphaelitism of the 1850s in his *Art of England* lectures (1883), exhorting his listeners never to "confuse a Myth with a lie" (Cook & Wedderburn, xxxiii, 293).
37 See Nunn, 1995, ch.7.
38 Staley in Casteras and Denny, 1996, 70-1.
39 *Athenaeum*, 25 May 1889, 669.
40 *The Saturday Review*, 13 May 1893, 511.
41 21 May 1892, 672.
42 'The Lay Figure', 1898, 70.
43 Dixon, 1902, 256.
44 Rose, 27.
45 *Times*, 8 March 1927, 21.
46 McAllister, 1920, 29.

# Catalogue and Biographies

## Entries compiled by Pamela Gerrish Nunn and Jan Marsh

**Sizes are in centimetres, height before width.**

**Abbreviations**

| | |
|---|---|
| **s** signed | **d** dated |
| **inscr** inscribed | **init** initialled |
| **priv. coll.** private collection | **cat** catalogue |

Sources cited are fully listed in the bibliography.

## Barbara Leigh Smith
### *later* Bodichon

*Barbara Bodichon, courtesy of the Mistress and Fellows of Girton College, Cambridge*

Born 1827 in Sussex, daughter of Radical MP Benjamin Leigh Smith, and eldest of five illegitimate children; cousin to Florence Nightingale. Her father's settlement of a personal income of £300 p.a. at age 21 allowed her exceptional opportunities, devoted to art and social reform. She wrote journalism and verse from 1848 and with poet Bessie Parkes travelled unchaperoned in 1850, visiting Anna Howitt and Jane Benham Hay [q.v.] in Munich. Encouraged by Howitt, Bodichon took instruction from William Henry Hunt, John Varley, and later Camille Corot, Charles Daubigny and Hercules Brabazon; her exhibition debut was in 1850. Reform was as important as art, however, and with other women she formed what is now known as the Langham Place Group to campaign for women's rights, including reform of married women's property laws. In 1858 launched the feminist *Englishwoman's Journal*. In 1857 married Eugene Bodichon, French doctor and social reformer, afterwards visiting sites of sociopoliticial interest in the USA. Thenceforth they spent half the year in Algeria, leading to specialisation in her art in North African landscape (e.g. *Sisters Working in our Fields* [cat.4]). In 1861, at the first of several solo exhibitions in London, she showed mainly landscape watercolours.

During her career she appeared at the RA, the French Gallery, SFA, SBA, BI, Glasgow, Dudley, NI, Crystal Palace, Birmingham, Liverpool, the International Exhibition 1872 and commercial galleries, notably that of the prominent dealer Gambart. Her significance to the women artists' movement was acknowledged in the critical appellation "the Rosa Bonheur of landscape". In 1865, the Langham Place Group campaigned for women's suffrage with John Stuart Mill, and in 1869 their efforts towards higher education for women brought the foundation of Girton College, Cambridge. Bodichon won Crystal Palace medals for art in 1873, 1877, 1878. In 1877 she suffered a stroke from which she never fully recovered. Her last recorded exhibition occurred in 1881, and she died at her home near Hastings in June 1891.

**1 Dreams of Escape: Ireland 1846.** c.1846
watercolour and bodycolour, with varnish on paper
23 x 33
Whitworth Art Gallery, University of Manchester

This drawing is amongst Bodichon's earliest surviving work and unexhibited during her lifetime.

It was made in a sketch book in use from 1846 to 1851 which has since been dismembered; other subjects in this album included

family portraits, copies of contemporary artists' work, a Shakespearean scene and a sketch of Scottish peasants. This piece, presumably made in 1846, was no doubt provoked by the famine in Ireland that year and informed by a visit she had made with her family in 1845: "This year they were in Ireland and next year I expect they will go to Italy. Their father dotes on them. They take with them books and sketching materials", reported the writer Mary Howitt ( Burton, 4)

The sociopolitical subject "from the days when her girlish thoughts deepened into reflection" (Clayton, ii, 168) signals the artist's burgeoning concern with the kind of matters that were to animate her whole adult life. The transparent use of the Romantic style - hints of both Francis Danby and J.M.W. Turner are evident here - indicates that she had not yet been convinced that Realism was the modern vehicle for social commentary. But the power developed by Pre-Raphaelitism - introduced to the artist by Anna Mary Howitt shortly after the date of this drawing - to picture contemporary issues is presaged by the vividness and earnestness of this work, private and unpolished as it is.

The ships' masts in the right background may be left from an earlier sketch made on this page, but, taken with the drawing's title pencilled in the sketchbook, suggest the emigration that offered the only relief for thousands of hard-pressed Irish peasants at this time.

### 2 Elizabeth Siddal 1854
s & d 'Scalands May 8th 1854 / Barbara L Smith'
pencil on paper
12.5 x 9.5
Mark Samuels Lasner

Elizabeth Siddal was a Pre-Raphaelite model and in 1854 at the outset of her career as artist. While staying at Hastings, she visited the Leigh Smith country estate Scalands, near Robertsbridge. "My dear Miss Smith," she wrote on 4 May. "This morning I received a letter from Rossetti who will be here  tomorrow or Friday. Shall we come over and see you and Miss Howitt?" (Princeton). The visit followed on 8 May, when she sat informally to the three fellow artists [cat.5 and fig.18]. "Barbara Smith, Miss Howitt and I made sketches of her

dear head with iris stuck in her dear hair" wrote Rossetti to his brother (Doughty and Wahl, 159).The artist was introduced to the sitter early in 1854, when she told a friend she was taking "a strong interest in a young girl formerly model to Millais and Dante Rossetti, now Rossetti's love and pupil..." (Girton). All three portraits made on this occasion were retained by Bodichon and inherited by her heirs. Bodichon's sketch illustrates her preference for catching a likeness or a landscape swiftly.

### 3 At Ventnor, Isle of Wight 1856
inscr 'Leigh Smith / Ventnor IoW / 1856'
watercolour and bodycolour, with scratching out on paper
71 x 107 (arched top)
Private Collection
Manchester and Birmingham showings only

In January 1856, the artist was staying with Howitt at Ventnor on the south coast of the Isle of Wight, for the express purpose of landscape painting. On 14 January she wrote to her friend Marian Evans (George Eliot) "Anna Mary read to me as we sat together in our studio overhanging the stormy sea after our day's painting." (Girton). This sea and cliff view was exhibited at the RA (no.913) later the same year together with *The Seagrove* (no.800) and *The Margin of the Sea* (no.964).

The artist had family connections with the Isle of Wight, which was also popular with artists owing to its coastal landscape. Another nearby view is seen in Boyce's *Shanklin* [cat.18].

At this date Bodichon and Howitt were working closely together. "Anna Mary says my little oils are very good for first productions from nature. My landscape is very PRB," she had written in 1854 (Girton). Landscape was Bodichon's preferred genre, and this large example demonstrates her vigorous response to, and conceptual grasp of, Pre-Raphaelitism. In his report on the 1856 Crystal Palace exhibition, W.M. Rossetti mentioned a "capital" coast scene by Miss Barbara Smith, "full of real PreRaphaelitism" (*Crayon*, August 1856, 245) which suggests that *At Ventnor* was typical of her exhibition production at this date. The following year the same critic described Bodichon as an artist "of great power" who was also "well known as a woman who writes and exerts herself for public objects." (Yale).

**4 Sisters Working in our Fields** c. 1858-60
watercolour and body colour on paper
25 x 46
John Crabbe

While painting with Anna Mary Howitt on the Isle of Wight in 1856 [see cat.3], the artist wrote to George Eliot: "I must go to some wilder country to paint - because I believe I shall paint well" (14 January 1856, Yale). Only eight months later, she made her first visit to North Africa and, though this drawing gives a peaceful picture of a domesticated land, Algeria does seem to have been the place she believed might fit the bill. "[T]he foreground of wild olives, ruins of mills, old moorish mosques and houses with their constant companions the tall cypress trees make pictures - this is what strikes one - here are all the subjects really combined - here are the ideals real which painters have been trying to paint since landscape art began...", she wrote to Bessie Parkes (see Orr, 180). The scene shown here is from the "villa on the green heights of Mustapha Supérieur, commanding a glorious view of sea, city, and plain" (Clayton, ii, 172), which the Bodichons bought on their marriage in 1858.

Algerian landscapes quickly became Barbara Bodichon's speciality. Her first appearance at the SFA (1858) was with five Algerian landscapes; and Algerian scenes were the principal subject of her solo exhibitions in April-May 1861 (French Gallery), summer 1864 (French Gallery), July 1865 and (with Eliza Bridell-Fox) July 1866 (German Gallery). Here the artist's technique has broadened, perhaps as a consequence of less frequent contact with Howitt and other Pre-Raphaelites. As Deborah Cherry observes (in West), drawings like this, though part of Bodichon's effort to create a feminist relationship with this country, cannot escape a connection with Orientalism's objectification of the exotic.

# Anna Mary Howitt
## *later* Watts

Born in Nottingham in 1824, daughter of William and Mary Howitt, a well-known Radical and literary couple. In 1840-3 the family lived in Germany to benefit from the educational system. Having shown precocious talent in art, she attended Sass's school in London and public lectures at the Royal Academy. Influenced by German painting and idealism, in 1850-2 she studied in Munich with Jane Benham Hay, receiving informal supervision from Wilhelm von Kaulbach (1805-74); her account of this experience was published as *An Art Student in Munich* (1853, reprinted 1880). Other writings of this period include two serial stories, "*The School of Life*" (1853) whose protagonist is a young male artist, and "*Sisters in Art*" (1853) which elaborated the aspirations of the new generation of women artists. With Bodichon and other friends, formed a group of young feminists that laid the ground for the later Langham Place group. On friendly terms with members of the Pre-Raphaelite Brotherhood, Howitt participated in the short-lived Folio Club in 1854, and was invited to write as a Pre-Raphaelite for *The Crayon* (New York). Her exhibition debut was at the National Institution in 1854 with a depiction of Margaret from Faust (untraced) which attracted attention. This was followed by *The Castaway* (RA 1855, unlocated), *The Sensitive Plant* (1855 [fig. 9]) and *Boadicea* (Crystal Palace, 1856, untraced), all indicative of social and feminist concerns. The rejection of the last by the RA, together with Ruskin's criticism of it, following the end of her engagement to engraver Edward Bateman, preceded a mental breakdown, causing Howitt to destroy her pictures and abandon public ambition, her only subsequent exhibit being at the SFA in 1857. In 1859 she married Alaric A. Watts, with whom she shared a deep immersion in spiritualism, which thenceforth claimed her creativity. From 1870 the couple lived in Cheyne Walk, Chelsea, close to artists including Rossetti and William Bell Scott. She died in Germany in 1884.

**5 Elizabeth Siddal** 1854
inscr 'Scalands / May 8th'
pencil on paper
12.7 x 11.5
Mark Samuels Lasner

A companion piece to Bodichon's portrait [cat.2], made on the same occasion when Howitt was staying at Bodichon's country home on the Kent-Sussex border. On 8 May 1854, Elizabeth Siddal, who had met the Howitts in London, visited from Hastings with D.G. Rossetti, and sat for the others wearing iris flowers in her hair.

Complementing Siddal's own works in the present exhibition [cats. 20-26], the drawing demonstrates the links between the women artists associated with the movement, and is a valuable survivor insofar as virtually all works by Howitt have disappeared apart from the 1853 diptych *The Sensitive Plant* [fig.9]. Howitt's interpretation of Siddal's features shows the influence of the German school she admired, while the sitter's expression chimes with a later comment by Bessie Parkes, that Siddal was "a remarkably retiring English girl [who] had the look of one who read her Bible and said her prayers every night" (Rose, 7).

Fig.18
D.G. Rossetti, *Elizabeth Siddal*, unlocated, photograph couresy of the Mistress and Fellows of Girton College, Cambridge

Both this and cat.2 compare with the numerous portrait drawings of Siddal, Pre-Raphaelitism's first icon, made by Rossetti at this date, such as fig.18 (Surtees, 1991). The hair decorated with "natural ornament" reflects contemporary fashion.

# Rosa Brett

*Rosa Brett,* family photograph

Born 1829 in Camberwell, but spent her childhood in Dublin, where her father was posted as army surgeon. The oldest of four children, she had three brothers. The family probably moved to the Manchester area in the early 1840s but by 1850 settled in Kent, Mrs Brett's birthplace, where Rosa lived until her death. She was essentially self-taught alongside her brother John, devoting herself to the study of nature from 1850. John became a well-known Pre-Raphaelite landscape painter and encouraged his sister in her art, sharing his expertise and acquaintance with her. During 1854-5 she was seriously ill and spent time in Belgium, whether for cure or convalescence is unknown. Her first exhibition in 1858, with *The Hayloft* [fig. 8] was under the masculine pseudonym Rosarius, which she retained until 1862. This, and the fact that she could spend only sporadic periods in London mixing with other artists because of her domestic obligations as an unmarried daughter, may have hindered her progress, as she appears to have sold little work and never gained a reputation though she continued to draw and paint throughout her life. During her career, she appeared with oils and watercolours of landscapes and animal studies at RA, SLA, Manchester, Liverpool. Brett's last recorded exhibition was in 1881, a year in which she also spent a period sketching in Wales. She died in Surrey in July 1882.

**6 From Bluebell Hill** 1851
s & d 'Brett 1851'; on mount, 'Sketched from Bluebell Hill'
watercolour on paper
11.4 x 18
Private Collection

This watercolour, never exhibited in her lifetime, was made on one of the numerous sketching sessions which the artist and her brother John were in the habit of making almost daily when the weather suited to sites around their home in Detling, near Maidstone, Kent. Bluebell Hill is about four miles north-east of the artist's home, a prominent rise looking down over the Pilgrim's Way and Kit's Coty, the

megalithic tomb shown in her later sketchbook [cat. 10b]. Though all the places they depicted lay within a five-mile radius, their excursions varied from a whole day to a couple of hours, depending very much, in Rosa's case, on domestic duties. An outing such as that which produced the present drawing is described in the artist's unpublished diary. "Dined and went to sketch at same place as yesterday ... returned home after sunset very tired indeed, the distance being rather long, the weather hot and roads hilly, got 2 sketches. " (22 August 1851).

This motif clearly attracted Brett. *Evening Close to Detling* (priv. coll.) was made within the same year. Similar ingredients can be seen also in the much larger watercolour of 1869, *Barming (Kentish Cornfields after Sunset)* (priv. coll.) in which the vivid hues of the sky at the end of the day form a poetical setting for workers returning home along a Kentish lane.

### 7 In the Artist's Garden   c.1859-60
oil on board, unfinished
15.6 x 14.2
David Dallas

It is not known why this painting is uncompleted, since it was clearly being worked to an exhibitable level of finish. It shows the blossoming chestnut, lilac and lawn of the garden of the house in Detling where the artist lived with her family from c.1851 until around 1861, and probably dates from 1859-60. Detling appears in a finished work of 1858, *Detling Church* (priv. coll.), of comparable style, and a note in a letter of May 1859 records the artist painting horse-chestnut blossoms, which are prominent in the present work. In June of that year, she went visiting to Devon, which may explain the abandonment of this painting. Indeed, the work hints in all its defining aspects - its unfinished state, its small scale, its subject matter, the intensity of its observation and the enclosed space it portrays - at the relentless inhibition of Brett's vocation by family, domesticity and social convention.

Though unfinished, it shows several of the well-known and characteristic Pre-Raphaelite techniques: vivid colour applied to a white ground; all-over or 'democratic' focus, with each area of the image given the same amount of attention; detail of natural growth in the trees, blossoms and grass; on-the-spot observation of nature, revealed especially in the realism of the grass and the play of sunlight on the entire scene. These are elements of 'classic' Ruskinian Pre-Raphaelitism.

### 8 The Old House at Farleigh   1862
s & d RB 1862
oil on canvas
35.5  x  49.4
Private Collection

Though this, the artist's largest known work, is made on exhibition scale, there is no record of its exhibition during her lifetime and it has remained in the Brett family. Family correspondence records that it was begun on 10 July 1862 and completed by the autumn. It depicts one of Kent's many extant medieval houses, the Manor House at the village of East Farleigh, about two miles south-west of Maidstone, off the Tonbridge Road, where the

Fig.19
*East Farleigh Manor House*, RCHME © Crown Copyright

artist lived in 1862. This building, more properly known as the Court Lodge, was the manor house of East Farleigh belonging to Christ Church Priory, Canterbury. Its stone parts probably date from the late 13th or early 14th century, while the timber range may have been built two hundred years later. Writing in 1798, Edward Hasted noted in his *History and Topographical Survey of the County of Kent* that "it has not been inhabited but by cottagers for many years; a great part of it seems to have been pulled down, and the remains make but a very mean appearance" (Hasted, 1972, 377). The house was pulled down in 1874 and the half-timbered wing rebuilt in Maidstone as part of the town's museum.

Such a local landmark, worked and presented so elaborately, must either have been a commission or a determined attempt to win exhibition at the Academy, where Brett had experienced mixed success since 1858. It appears that it succeeded on neither score, impressive though it is as an example of the persistence of Ruskinian Pre-Raphaelitism during the 1860s.

*Our thanks to Sarah Pearson for assistance in compiling this entry.*

**9 Bunny** 1873
inscr 'Portrait of Bunny 18th. May 1873 RB'
pencil on paper
12 x 13.5
Private Collection

This study of the artist's cat is one of several fine animal and bird studies that remain from her hand, made through-

out her career. Others are of chicks, rabbits and mice (priv. colls.). While this drawing would not have been meant for exhibition, it is a complete work suff-icient unto itself. There is no evid-ence that it was used as preparation for a painting, and the artist's inscription suggests her satisfaction with it in the present state. It recalls her first success, now lost, the painting *The Hayloft* [fig. 8], which in 1858 formed Brett's first appearance at the Academy. Despite the slightness of the present work, it is clear from descriptions of *The Hayloft* that, twenty years later, Brett had lost neither her affectionate insight into animal habit and form nor her minute touch. "There is an astonishing cat, dozing in tabby comfort... how hard she blinks her green eyes, and with what inward satisfaction she tucks up her fore paws upon her litter of hay in the out-house! For minute picking out of every detail of fur, its softness and its gloss, this little picture is quite a phenomenon." (*Spectator*, 5 June 1858, 624).

**10 Sketchbooks**
**(a)1871-2 sketchbook**
**(b)1876-9 sketchbook**
pencil on paper
(a)  15.3 x 24.3 open 490
(b)  15.3 x 24 open 475
On loan from the National Maritime Museum, Greenwich

These sketchbooks show the artist as a keen student of nature throughout her life, remaining a Pre-Raphaelite in the Ruskinian sense for the duration of her career. They were used by the artist for sketching and studying outdoors in the 1870s. **(a)** dates from 1871 to 1872, while **(b)** was used over three years from 1876 to 1879. Their contents range from scraps of observation to complete scenes studied in detail with colour notes and aides memoires as preparation for a painting.

Sketchbook (a), inscribed May 25 1871, shows a study typical of the contents of this book, an unidentified group of trees, annotated with observations such as "small patch of bright green" and "this is lost amongst foliage of near trees". It exhibits the same fidelity to nature as Brett's early painting, *In the Artist's Garden* [cat. 7]. The scene recorded in (b) has been identified as Kit's Coty, a megalithic burial chamber near the village of Aylesford, two miles north of Maidstone. The name Kit's Coty derives from a Celtic phrase meaning 'tomb in the woods'. As in (a), the artist has made notes for herself of materials, textures and colours that suggest the intention of making a later painting. Had this been accomplished, the work would have compared with *The Old House at Farleigh* [cat. 8] as an attempt to exploit the appeal of Kent's historic landscape with the gallery-going public. Other pages in this book show local sights, such as hop-pickers at the hopping bins, and nature studies such as those that predominate in sketchbook (a).

# Anna Blunden
## *later* Martino

*Anna Blunden*

Born London in December 1829, daughter of a bookbinder; both parents established themselves in the artificial flower and straw hat trade after the family moved to Blunden's mother's birthplace, Exeter, in 1833, where two younger sisters were born. After working as a governess in Torquay 1852-3, Blunden turned to art as a more congenial way of earning a living. Blunden was self-taught by copying at the British Museum and National Gallery, with slight attendance at Leigh's and informal instruction from Ruskin, whom she approached for advice in 1855 and with whom she had a long correspondence. She first exhibited in 1854 at the SBA, with the topical social subject *For only one short hour...*[cat. 11]. Other genre pictures followed, taking up current themes (*The Emigrant*, 1855, untraced; *Uncle Tom's Cabin*, [fig.15]). Through Ruskin procured some commissions in late 1850s and, while trying to make her mark in London, she ran a portrait practice and teaching studio in· Exeter. This situation continued from 1856 to 1867. During her career, she appeared firstly with oil paintings and later also with watercolours at RA, SBA, BI, SFA, Dudley, Liverpool, Birmingham, Glasgow, Exeter, Crystal Palace. During the 1860s she turned increasingly to landscape. Blunden travelled on the Continent in the years 1867-72, having a studio in Rome in 1870. In 1872, she married her deceased sister's husband, becoming Mrs Martino and stepmother to his children. Because such a marriage was illegal in Britain, the wedding took place abroad, but later obfuscation by Blunden prevents us from knowing whether it was in Italy or Germany. On their return to England, they settled in Birmingham where a daughter was born in 1874. Blunden published pamphlets on social topics from 1877 onwards, while continuing to exhibit; her last recorded exhibition was in 1915, the year of her death. Though a prolific artist, she is now poorly represented as many of her works were destroyed in Exeter in the Second World War.

## 11 'For only one short hour' (Song of the Shirt)
1854
oil on canvas
47 x 39.5
Yale Center for British Art, Paul Mellon Fund

This modern-life subject was exhibited in 1854, with the quotation, "For only one short hour / to feel as I used to feel / before I knew the woes of want / and the walk that costs a meal", from Thomas Hood's poem on the plight of underpaid seamstresses *The Song of the Shirt*, published in 1843 and one of the best-known poems of its time. The garment-making trade was exposed by Hood's poem for its exploitation of female homeworkers and the running of sweatshops which were likewise reliant on female labour. The scandal was the greater for the revelation that middle-class women fallen on hard times were drawn into the ranks of such needlewomen (see Edelstein).

This painting formed the artist's exhibition debut at the SBA, and heralds her adoption of social realist painting, begun by Richard Redgrave in the 1840s and boosted by Pre-Raphaelitism's enthusiasm for contemporary issues as fit subject matter for a meaningful modern art. Along with the governess, the poor seamstress in her garret became a familiar figure within Realism. Blunden's treatment can be compared with those of John Everett Millais, Charles Cope, George Hicks, Frank Holl, Louise Jopling, Edward Radford and Charles Eastlake, all deriving essentially from Richard Redgrave's *The Sempstress* (1846, Forbes Magazine Collection). This work was included (no. 13) in the exhibition of British Art in 1857-8 that introduced the Pre-Raphaelite movement to US audiences.

The artist's other works in this vein include *Uncle Tom's Cabin* (undated, Sotheby's 1977) [fig. 15], *The Emigrant* (SBA 1855, presumed destroyed), *The Sister of Mercy* (RA, 1856, presumed destroyed) and *The Daguerreotype* (RA, 1857, presumed destroyed). This is a rare surviving example of the figure work with which Blunden first came to critical attention.

**12 View near the Lizard: Polpeor Beach** 1862
s & d A. Blunden 1862
watercolour heightened with white on paper
32.9 x 56.6
Whitworth Art Gallery, University of Manchester

Though Blunden began her exhibiting career with genre paintings, in 1859 she turned to landscape and by the mid 1860s was well known as a landscapist in oil and watercolour. The present work is one of several Cornish landscapes she exhibited between 1863 and 1868 (e.g. *Kynance Cove, Cornwall* [RA 1863], *Mullion Cove* [RA 1864], *On the Cliffs at Mullion* [Dudley, 1865], *Tintagel* [RA 1867]; all unlocated), and is here identified as *Polpeor Beach*, shown at the autumn exhibition in Birmingham in 1865 and offered for exhibition in Greenock the following year as *Poll Pier Beach at the Lizard*. The distinctive Lizard

lighthouse with its two hexagonal towers, built in 1751 and altered after the date of this drawing (1903) hovers like a vision in the sunlight above Polpeor Cove (its correct name) which lies almost due east of Lizard Point.

Blunden had clearly taken seriously the judgement of Ruskin, whose advice she sedulously sought between 1855 and 1863. In a letter which Virginia Surtees has dated to May 1862, Ruskin wrote: "You have a power of colouring which I have rarely seen equalled, and great dexterity of execution and truth of eye. You ought to be able to produce immediately saleable pictures, and that for high prices. You are at present hindered from doing this by a want of taste, for which I cannot account - though it arises partly from want of education. It tells quite fatally and absolutely without hope against your figure subjects. You must give figures up at once, you will never be able to sell one. In landscape let someone else - any popular hack of an artist - choose your subjects. He may choose you three or four - and you may choose the one you like best - then paint it honestly and it will sell" (Surtees, 1972, letter B.94).

Blunden was evidently directed to the south-west of England, for in 1862 her address was given in the Liverpool exhibition catalogue as The Lizard. Her efforts bore fruit, as the *Times* commented at the 1864 RA, "Seashore pictures abound, and Cornwall and North Devon are favourite 'pitches'

for this kind of subject. One of the best of these pictures is Miss Blunden's *Mullion Cove*" (18 May 1864, 10). With this kind of work, Blunden became connected by critics with John Brett, a better known protegé of Ruskin, whose marine landscape paintings always attracted critical attention. "In his own peculiar line, Miss Blunden comes not far behind him," wrote the *Spectator's* reviewer at the 1864 RA (18 June 1864, 711). Though Blunden continued to produce landscapes for the rest of her career, only a handful are presently known.

# Jane Benham
## *later* Benham Hay

Born December 1829, daughter of an ironmonger whose position improved considerably during her childhood. She first exhibited in 1848 but left England to study in Munich with Anna Mary Howitt in May 1850. Married in 1851 to artist William Hay, Benham Hay became a mother in 1852. She produced illustrative work from 1853, much of it for Henry Vizetelli, leading publisher of illustrated literature, and a children's storybook, *The Three Boys*, that appeared in December 1854. In 1857 or earlier, she moved to Italy, being sympathetic to the cause of Italian independence. She made a successful return to the RA in 1859 with *England and Italy* [cat. 13], attracting attention over the next several years with figurative compositions from historical, Biblical and literary sources which made increasing reference to Italian history, culture and politics (e.g. *The Reception of the Prodigal Son*, 1862, Russell-Cotes Art Gallery, Bournemouth). During her career she appeared at RA, Liverpool, SFA, and the French Gallery. She lived in Florence until at least 1867, becoming acquainted with British expatriates and visitors such as George Eliot and George Lewes. Benham Hay achieved her greatest success in 1867 with *The Florentine Procession* known as *The Burning of the Vanities* [fig.6] (Homerton College, Cambridge), exhibited by Henry Wallis at the French Gallery, London. Her last recorded exhibition was in 1887, when her chef d'oeuvre from 1867 was shown at Liverpool. She is thought to have died in Italy. She certainly lost contact with old acquaintances; in 1895, Bessie Parkes did not even know whether Benham Hay was still alive.

**13 England and Italy** 1859
s & d 'J.E. Benham Hay 1859 Florence' with
Florentine lily; on back of frame 'Liberty Equality
Fraternity'
oil on canvas
46.4 x 80
Dr Mark Hirsh and Mrs Jane C. Hirsh

This canvas was presented in the 1859 Royal Academy catalogue as "Two boys, one of English type, the other an Italian boy of the people". Stating that the work was painted in the Val d'Arno in 1859, the artist went on to say: "In one I have endeavoured to express the pure happiness of our children; in the other the obstination of the oppressed and suffering poor of Italy".

The subject of the relationship between England and Italy was highly topical, with the struggle between those who desired the unification of Italy locked in political conflict with supporters of the Austro-Hungarian empire that dominated the Italian states. Shortly before the Academy of 1859 opened, the French had liberated northern Italy by defeating the Austrian army at Magenta and during the exhibition an armistice was signed between the French and the Austrians leading eventually to the installation of the unificationists' hero Garibaldi as interim dictator in September 1860.

The *Times*, which believed the artist to be a Mr Hay, found "a rare truth in the landscape" spoiled by the figures' injection of social comment (30 April 1859, 12). This same combination of sentiments was expressed in *The Examiner*, which truculently refused the political allegory. "England and Italy is à remarkably well painted work, intended to mean something but meaning nothing. A sentimentally fair little gentleman from England is contrasted with an Italian ragamuffin. Will Mrs Hay contrast next year, in a companion work, the child of an Italian lady with a little Wiltshire scarecrow, or some child of the gutter picked up in an English town? If it be meant to suggest among other things rich England and poor Italy, then there is a pretension of completeness in the parallel which can only make the want of true point in the study more conspicuous." (4 June 1859, 358). Some observers preferred Benham's accompanying exhibit, *A Boy in Florentine Costume of the*

*15th Century* (Sotheby's 1977) [fig. 10], which featured the model for 'England' (perhaps the artist's son) wandering in a pleasant Tuscan landscape.

Though many artists were sympathetic to the cause of Italian independence, few seem to have introduced the issue into the London galleries. Certainly, neither Hunt's literary *Rienzi* (1849, priv. coll.) nor William Gale's genre piece *Naples, 1859* (1861, unlocated) achieved the topicality of *England and Italy*. Benham's work reflects her acquaintance with the radical circle which included the Friends of Italy Society (1851-6) and the activist Jessie White (later Mario), and displays the artist's varied links. The Pre-Raphaelite echoes of Ford Madox Brown's *The Pretty Baa-Lambs* (1851-3 and 1859, Birmingham Museum and Art Gallery) and John Brett's *The Stonebreaker* (1858, Liverpool, Walker Art Gallery) sound alongside that of the French Realist Gustave Courbet's *The Stonebreakers* (1851) which Benham Hay may have seen in the Salon of 1850-1, or in 1855 in the independent exhibition Courbet mounted at the time of the Paris International Exposition. In addition, the Nazarene painter Friedrich Overbeck's *Italy and Germany* (1828, Neue Pinakothek, Munich) suggests itself as an appropriate model which the artist is likely to have seen in Munich. A tantalising anticipation of Ruskin's figure of the two boys, Giorgione and Turner, in the fifth volume of *Modern Painters*, which appeared in 1860, remains to be investigated.

Benham Hay's independence of approach perhaps hindered its sale, for *England and Italy* was sent to the Liverpool Autumn Exhibition later the same year, along with its companion from the Academy, still for sale. Furthermore, *England and Italy* was still in the artist's possession in 1861 for in March 1861 George Eliot told Barbara Bodichon that she had seen the artist's works in London, saying "[o]ne of these - a view near Florence with a foreground of stones (exhibited the year before last) - pleased me highly" (Haight, 1975-8, iii, 388). A later Academy exhibit, *A Study of Stones in the Val d'Arno* (1862, unlocated), can be assumed to be related to the present painting.

# Joanna Mary Boyce *later* Wells

Born in London December 1831. Her father was a wine merchant until 1842, when he became a pawnbroker. Of her two brothers and two sisters, the oldest, George, also became an artist. Boyce showed artistic talent during childhood and enrolled at Cary's in 1849, moving in 1852 to Leigh's after a six month hiatus in 1850 to nurse George through serious illness.

J.H. Foley, *Portrait Bust of Joanna Boyce,* 1862, Private Collection

A holiday in Paris in April 1852 with her father developed her knowledge of art, though his death the following year set her back. She attended the Government School of Design in 1854, becoming acquainted at that time with progressive women such as Anna Mary Howitt and Jane Benham Hay and, through George, the male Pre-Raphaelites. Her first exhibition, *Elgiva* [cat. 14], at the 1855 RA was noticed by Ruskin, and she went on to exhibit again at RA, SBA, the French Gallery, and Liverpool. In September 1855 she went to the Paris studio of Thomas Couture, having been dissuaded from her preference for Rosa Bonheur by her suitor Henry Wells, a portrait painter. Her stay was truncated by ill health, but Boyce was invited by an editor friend of the family to review that year's Exposition Universelle Salon (*Saturday Review,* December 1855), and the next year's Royal Academy (*Saturday Review,* May-June 1856), an unusual opportunity for a woman. In 1857, she toured France and Italy with Henry Wells, whom she married in Rome in December; this trip resulted in her next major work, *The Child's Crusade* (RA 1860, priv. coll). On return to Britain in March 1858, the couple resided in Surrey while retaining a London studio. Their children Sidney, Alice and Joanna Margaret were born in quick succession, a circumstance their mother made use of in the production of portraits and domestic genre such as *Peep Bo!* (1861, destroyed) and *Sidney Wells* [1859, cat. 15]. She did illustrative work in 1859, indicating the financial pressures of a growing family. Joanna Boyce died after giving birth to her third child, in July 1861, leaving unfinished works such as *Gretchen* [cat. 19] and *A Sibyl* (priv. coll.) and many unfulfilled plans for further pictures. Her work was shown in the International Exhibition 1862, in a representative selection at the RA in 1901 and a memorial exhibition at the Tate Gallery in 1935. Several important works were destroyed during Second World War bombing of Bath.

## 14 Elgiva 1855
oil on canvas
50.8 x 40.8
Private Collection

Elgiva was an Anglo-Saxon noblewoman who, according to David Hume's *History of England* (1754-7), fell foul of the powerful Archbishop Odo. Her marriage was forcibly dissolved, she was branded on the face and exiled to Ireland.

This was the artist's first exhibited work. The painting was widely praised and seen to mark the arrival of a new talent.

In a supplement to his *Academy Notes* of this year, Ruskin praised the subtle and tender rendering of the head's expression. "As we watch the face for a little time, the slight arch of the lip seems to begin to quiver, and the eyes fill with ineffable sadness and on-look of despair", he wrote. "The dignity of all the treatment - the beautiful imagination of faint but pure colour, place this picture, to my mind, among those of the very highest power and promise" (Cook and Wedderburn, xiv, 31). In his diary, Ford Madox Brown complimented Boyce's exhibit as "the best head in the rooms" (Surtees 1981, 22 May 1855). The embodiment of a moral subject in an English heroine provides an understandable object of admiration for both these men, though, in its evocation of the art of the Swiss painter Ary Scheffer, *Elgiva* evidences the artist's independence of vision.

The choice of subject, treated by Millais in 1847 in a painting showing Elgiva being seized by Odo's men (Birmingham Museum and Art Gallery), but otherwise obscure, may be compared with Boyce's *Rowena* (destroyed), prepared for the following year's Academy but not accepted, and Howitt's *Boadicea* of 1856 (unlocated). All represent heroic female figures from English history who comment inevitably on the contemporary debate on the role of women. Another point of reference is the American sculptor Harriet Hosmer's *Zenobia* (1859, Wadsworth Athenaeum), a subject which Boyce herself was planning to tackle at the time of her unexpected death [see cat. 16].

*Elgiva* was not purchased from the 1855 Academy, though it appeared at the Liverpool exhibition in 1858 marked "sold", and was bought in early 1859 by the artist's brother George. It has remained in the Boyce family ever since.

**15 Portrait of Sidney Wells**   1859
s with monogram JMW '59
oil on canvas
27.6 x 25.1
Tate Gallery. Presented by Anne Christopherson 1996 to celebrate the Tate Gallery Centenary 1997

Sidney was the artist's first child, born at the end of 1858 and pictured here while less than a year old. "Baby does possess an exiguous beauty of form, too exiguous perhaps. I want sadly to paint him, but is it possible?" Boyce wrote in her diary in September 1859. "I am trying to make a likeness of that little gentleman", she wrote to her friend Hennie in an undated letter of 1859, "but one might as well try to make a faithful study of a flea". Boyce bore two further children, both girls, but Sidney is the only one to have been so commemorated. His infancy is represented also in the genre scene *Peep-bo!* (1861, destroyed), which shows a mother, baby and nurse in a contemporary domestic interior. He died in 1869.

In format, this work builds on Boyce's earlier child heads such as *Little Red-Haired Boy (The Babbacombe Boy)* (1853, priv. coll.) and *Study of a Welch Boy* (1853, unlocated) but its minuteness of touch marks an intensification of her Pre-Raphaelitism. Though so highly finished and with the most direct appeal to the viewer, this arresting example of Pre-Raphaelite portraiture was rejected from the Academy and seems to have been unexhibited during the artist's lifetime. A remark

in Boyce's personal papers relating to her next major work *The Child's Crusade* (1860, priv. coll.) being badly hung, comments on *Sidney's* rejection from the Academy ("My poor Crusade! I only wish it had shared the fate of *Sidney* "[11 May 1860]). *Sidney's* absence from the appraisals of her work occasioned by Boyce's death, as well as from all posthumous showings of her work before the Tate Gallery tribute of 1935, suggest that this exquisite portrait was considered an especially personal work, an attitude perhaps consolidated by the sitter's and artist's untimely deaths.

**16 Head of Mrs Eaton**   1861
oil on paper laid on linen
17.1 x 13.7
Yale Center for British Art, Paul Mellon Fund

Perhaps the best documented of Boyce's surviving works, this head was made during the course of preparations for a major work, *A Sibyl*, unfinished at the artist's death and since destroyed (Nunn, 1993). The artist's papers contain elaborate technical notes made in November 1860 on "Small head  of Mrs. Eaton - on white hot pressed paper sketched in pencil carefully outlined black and firm - then scrubbed all over background and flesh transparent greenish brown".

Mrs Eaton was modelling at that time for several artists in the Pre-Raphaelite circle, including Rebecca Solomon, Simeon Solomon and Frederick Sandys. She was also employed by Albert Moore for his 1861 Academy exhibit, *The Mother of Sisera* (Carlisle, Tullie House Museum and Art Gallery), which comes closest to the present work in terms of format, means and effect. Closely related to both Moore's painting and the present work would have been the picture noted by Boyce in her future plans as "Life-sized head of Mrs. Eaton (Zenobia)".

This painting is yet another vivid demonstration of Boyce's very independent grasp of Pre-Raphaelitism. Black figures are infrequent in Pre-Raphaelite work and when the colleagues cited above did use Mrs Eaton, they tended to embed her features in a narrative or genre subject (see also Rossetti's later *The Beloved*, 1865, Tate Gallery), whereas Boyce treats her as an individual, the sitter for a portrait.

**17 Bird of God**     1861
s & d Joanna M. Wells 1861
oil on cardboard
21.2 x 20.6
Private Collection

"My Bird of God is finished or nearly so, but disappoints me sadly", wrote the artist in June 1861 to her friend Hennie, ever self-critical and aiming for the highest standard. This painting, inspired by Browning's poem *Guardian Angel*, became Boyce's last work on her unexpected death in July 1861, and as such attracted considerable attention. Some admirers referred to it as Seraph's Head. "Her last completed work - significantly enough - was a 'Seraph's Head', exalted and spiritual in sentiment, pure and melodious in colour", wrote Alexander Gilchrist art correspondent of *The Critic* (27 July 1861, 109). "Its execution seems to have called forth her utmost, as it has her latest, efforts. Full of the tenderest and most loving work...", hymned "Dry Point" in the *Spectator* (20 July 1861, 783). The painting appeared at the Academy in 1862, the year after the artist's death, while other works by Boyce were in the International Exhibition, attracting poignant praise. "An exquisite little picture of hers - her last labour - is in this exhibition, the head of a cherub, with soft brown hair, blown back, outspread wings, and white raiment", noted the *Times* reviewer (3 May 1862, 14).

*Bird of God* uses a model Boyce was employing also for a projected picture of Undine, an obvious successor to the children whose heads had formed the subject of works such as *Fair-haired Urchin* (1854, destroyed) and *Do I Like Butter?* (1861, priv. coll.). It also inevitably evokes the well-known *Angels' Heads* (1787, Tate Gallery) of the PRB's bête noire, Joshua Reynolds and may have suggested a motif to Julia Margaret Cameron (e.g. *I Wait*, 1872, RPS), and anticipates the later Pre-Raphaelite interest in angelic figures [see cat. 61]. Although reported by George Boyce as sold to

'Biggs, the dentist' in June 1861, *Bird of God* has remained in the artist's family and continued to represent Boyce in exhibition, being shown at the RA in 1901, the Whitechapel Art Gallery in 1905 and the Tate Gallery in 1935.

**18 Shanklin, Isle of Wight**   c.1860
oil on millboard
17.3 x 25
Private Collection

This is the only surviving example of Boyce's landscape painting, which formed an important subsidiary to the figure compositions and heads which dominated her output. It may well be one of the pieces the artist had in hand in the months following Sidney's birth, when she wrote to Hennie that she was preparing two landscapes for the Royal Academy, but "as I rarely get half an hour undisturbed they progress slowly". The absence of a signature suggests that Boyce may, indeed, have considered the work incomplete or unworthy of exhibition, and it has remained in the artist's family.

This painting indicates how within the early Pre-Raphaelite circle even those artists primarily drawn to figure painting recognised the importance of nature study. Boyce, of course, had in her brother George an example very close to hand of the power of landscape to absorb an artist. He, too, like many other painters [see cat. 3], found sites on the Isle of Wight.

**19 Gretchen**   1861
oil on canvas, unfinished
73 x 43.7
Tate Gallery.   Presented by the artist's daughters 1923

The subject is taken from Goethe's *Faust*, which served as inspiration for many artists within and beyond the Pre-Raphaelite circle. Margaret (Gretchen) is the innocent girl seduced and destroyed by Faust in Part One (originally published in 1808 and performed on the London stage in 1825), and Boyce lays her scene early in the story when, after being accosted in the street by Faust, the heroine is in her room alone in the evening, singing as she braids her hair. At the close of Part One, by which time Faust's attempts to ensnare her have developed apace, Margaret dies in prison, calling on God and the angels to save her soul. This seems to be the scene selected by Cameron for her *Gretchen at the Altar* (c. 1870) [fig. 13, p.72].

Some half-dozen pencil studies exist of the German nursemaid employed to look after the artist's children who served as the model for *Gretchen*. Dated around the end of January 1861, they attest to the careful planning of the pose, and the ultimate selection of the full-length standing figure indicates the confidence the artist had attained by this time. Boyce also had in hand at least two other ideas pivoting on full-length standing female figures, *Undine* and *A Sibyl* (sketches and studies in priv. coll.), suggesting that *Gretchen* typifies the kind of project she now planned to specialise in.

It is inevitable that this work should be compared with Boyce's friend Howitt's first success, *Margaret at the Fountain* (1854, unlocated), which Boyce noted in her diary as "not at all marvellous". Where Howitt chose a scene familiar from the numerous paintings from this source already exhibited, Boyce has chosen a less narrative, more monumental image upon whose ultimate power one can now only speculate. The interest of this figure for both Boyce and Howitt, however, is certain to have related to the corruption of female innocence by the self-seeking male, a theme seen within Pre-Raphaelitism in contemporary dress in Hunt's *The Awakening Conscience* (1853-4, Tate Gallery).

Presented to the national collection by the artist's daughters in 1923, *Gretchen*, commanding despite its unfinished state, is the artist's largest surviving work. It is, as Gilchrist wrote in his obituary notice, "perhaps the most eloquent indication of what the artist might have attained" (*The Critic*, 27 July 1861, 109).

# Elizabeth Eleanor Siddal
## *later* Rossetti

Elizabeth Siddal,
*Self Portrait 1853-4,* Private Collection

Born in London 1829, daughter of a cutler and small businessman from Sheffield. No details of her education are recorded but by age 20 Siddal was working as a milliner and dressmaker. Introduced to the PRB as a model, she sat to Walter Deverell, Holman Hunt and Millais. From 1852 she studied informally with Rossetti, who encouraged an earnest, naive style. In 1854 she met Bodichon and Howitt and in 1855 secured patronage from Ruskin, on whose allowance she visited Paris and Nice for the sake of her health. Her exhibition debut was at the Pre-Raphaelite salon at Russell Place in summer 1857, with drawings on literary subjects and a self-portrait in oils (priv. coll.); the watercolour *Clerk Saunders* [cat. 25] was also included in the British Art show that toured the USA. In 1857-8 Siddal visited Sheffield, where she made use of the art school facilities, and Matlock in Derbyshire. In May 1860, at a time of sickness, she married Rossetti and settled with him in London where she continued working, on romantic-medieval watercolours, assisting also with the decoration of William Morris's Red House and planning to collaborate on illustrations with Georgiana Burne-Jones. A stillborn daughter in 1861 was followed by post-natal depression and death from a laudanum overdose in February 1862. Later,

Rossetti re-collected her works and photographed her drawings and sketches, from which her ideas and output can be reconstructed. Subsequently her reputation as artist was wholly obscured by that as model, tragic muse, mistress and shrew, a process whose reversal began in 1984 with Siddal's token inclusion in the Tate Gallery show, and continued with the 1991 retrospective view of her work at the Ruskin Gallery Sheffield.

### 20 Pippa Passes    1854
s & d 'E.E.S. 54'
pen and brown ink over pencil on paper
23.4 x 29.8
The Visitors of the Ashmolean Museum, Oxford

This drawing illustrates scene III of *Pippa Passes* (1841) by Robert Browning, a dramatic poem set in the modern era, where the heroine, wandering through the city of Àsolo, passes a group of 'Poor Girls sitting on the steps' gossiping about their lovers and clients, rather as a young milliner in the 1850s might  encounter prostitutes in the London streets. One of the artist's earliest finished drawings, it was sold to Ruskin in 1855 and exhibited at the 1857 Pre-Raphaelite salon. In November 1855, it was shown to Browning by Rossetti, who reported that the poet was 'delighted beyond measure' (Doughty and Wahl, 227). In size and finish it forms a pair with *Lovers Listening to Music* of the same date [cat. 21].

Stylistically the work exemplifies the early Pre-Raphaelite taste for outline drawing and literary subjects, as seen in work by Millais, Hunt, Howitt, Charles Collins etc. Compositionally ambitious, it conveys the moral difference between Pippa and the group through the contrast of posture, clothing and expression. The theme relates to contemporary concerns with 'fallen' types of womanhood, as seen also in Hunt's *Awakening Conscience* (RA 1854, Tate Gallery ) and Rossetti's unfinished *Found* (1854, Delaware). Siddal's treatment offers a female perspective on the topic, suitably modified through the literary source, linking it to Howitt's lost works, *Margaret at the Fountain* (1854) and *The Castaway* (1855) as well as Boyce's *Gretchen* [cat. 19]. As an illustration to

Browning, it can be compared with Cameron's *Sordello* [cat. 37] and Brickdale's *I did no more...* [cat. 84]. Two other identical versions were made by the artist, perhaps with a view to further sales. The present work was acquired by the Ashmolean in 1977.

### 21 Lovers Listening to Music    1854
s & d 'E.E.S. 54'
pen and brown ink over pencil on paper
23.9 x 29.8
The Visitors of the Ashmolean Museum, Oxford

Described by W.M. Rossetti as 'Two lovers listening to the music of two dark Malay-looking women' (Burlington 1903, 278), the precise subject of this drawing has so far eluded identification, but is probably from a literary source. Just possibly it illustrates lines in one of the artist's own poems, "Love kept my heart in a song of joy / My pulses quivered to the tune; / The coldest blasts of winter blew / Upon it like sweet airs in June." (Marsh 1989, 208). Completed at around the same time  as cat. 20, the work's finished quality and adventurous subject attest to Siddal's professional ambitions and level of skill at the outset of her career.

The female figure would seem a self-image, comparable to that of Pippa in cat.20. W.M. Rossetti suggested that the male figure was drawn from his brother, in whose studio Siddal worked. A sketch dated 1853 (Birmingham Museum and Art Gallery) shows him sitting for her, in a reversal of the male artist / female model relation. The musicians and their instrument may well come from a published source, while the child, who presumably represents Love, is reminiscent of the angel in Rossetti's *Girlhood of Mary Virgin* (1849, Tate Gallery). The landscape background is thought to be studied from the Hastings area, where the artist stayed in spring 1854 [see cats.2 and 5].

A replica by the artist is now on loan to Wightwick Manor. One of the versions was made for William Allingham, to whom the original was promised, to replace that acquired by Ruskin in 1855 when he bought all Siddal's existing drawings (Doughty and Wahl, 245).

**22 Study for Lady Clare**   c.1854-5
pen and ink with brown and black wash over pencil
on paper
15 x 11.4
Lent by the Syndics of the Fitzwilliam Museum,
Cambridge

This heavily worked study for cat. 23 demonstrates the artist's working practices during the period of her closest association with Rossetti, when both chose small medievalised subjects set in enclosed spaces, depicting moments of dramatic emotion. As Deborah Cherry comments, "the drawing of the figures and the organisation of the architectural space oppose renaissance notions of anatomy and perspective which were enshrined in academic tradition" (Tate Gallery 1984, 222), the rejection of which was a Pre-Raphaelite principle in its early days.

The shape and scale of the drawing suggest it was begun as a prospective illustration, in response to the PRB commissions for the Moxon Tennyson. As such, it is representative of several similar sketches by the artist, recorded in a photographic portfolio compiled by her widower (Fitzwilliam). Subsequently, the work belonged to Frederick Leyland MP, and from 1892 to Charles Fairfax Murray, whose notes on the back record the work's soiled and torn condition at that date.

**23 Lady Clare**   1857
s & d 'EES / 57'
watercolour on paper
33.8 x 25.4
Private Collection

This drawing illustrates Tennyson's *Lady Clare* from *Poems* (1842), in which the heroine's natural mother begs her to conceal her humble origin, lest Lord Ronald withdraw his offer of marriage. Lady Clare refuses:

> 'If I'm a beggar born', she said,
> 'I will speak out, for I dare not lie.
> Pull off, pull off the brooch of gold
> And fling the diamond necklace by'.

> 'Nay now, my child,' said Alice the nurse,
> 'But keep the secret all ye can.'
> She said, 'Not so; but I will know
> If there be any faith in man.'

Inspired by her own liking for Tennyson (whose work she is first said to have seen in a newspaper) and by the 1857 edition of his *Poems* illustrated by Millais, Hunt, Rossetti and others, Siddal began several designs, including *St Cecilia* from *The Palace of Art* and *Jephtha's Daughter* from *A Dream of Fair Women*. *Lady Clare* is the only one completed, worked up from studies [see cat. 22] in a manner typical of 1850s Pre-Raphaelite practice.

The castle stairway and window reflect mid-Victorian interests in medieval art and architecture. Lady Clare's costume is derived from manuscript illustration seen by the artist in the British Museum. The stained glass scene of the Judgement of Solomon offers a typological reference to a scriptural moment when a true mother reveals herself.

The dramatic subject is also allusive to the specifically female concern, of being rejected by a prospective suitor on social or economic grounds, which may reflect a personal anxiety if Siddal feared her own marriage to Rossetti was impeded by class difference. As a theme of romantic fidelity, however - Lord Ronald does not reject a base-born bride - the work complements *Clerk Saunders* [cat. 25].

Included in the 1984 Tate Gallery exhibition (no. 222), *Lady Clare* was critically discussed there in relation to gender imagery, inter-textuality and Pre-Raphaelite compositional practice.

**24 The Ladies'
Lament from the
Ballad of Sir Patrick
Spens**   1856
s & d 'E.E.S / 1856'
watercolour on paper
24.1 x 22.9
Tate Gallery.
Purchased 1919

In the ballad of Sir Patrick Spens, the ladies of the Scottish court watch vainly for the return of their shipwrecked husbands, "O lang, lang may the ladies sit / With their fans into their hand / Or ever they see Sir Patrick Spens / Come sailing to the land."

In 1854 this ballad was selected by the artist from her copy of Walter Scott's *Minstrelsy of the Scottish Border* (Fitzwilliam) for illustration in an unrealised anthology to be edited by William Allingham (see Ruskin Gallery 1991, no.37). Like *Clerk Saunders* [cat. 25], it was subsequently worked up in watercolour, and is a characteristic example of Siddal's work, showing a complex figure group of women and children naively disposed in a coastal landscape.

During the lifetime of the artist's widower, the work hung in his house at Cheyne Walk. Subsequently, it belonged to his friend T. Watts-Dunton, and was purchased by the Tate Gallery in 1919.

### 25 Clerk Saunders   1857
s & d 'EES / 1857'
watercolour, bodycolour, and coloured chalks
on paper laid on stretcher
28.4 x 18.1
Lent by the Syndics of the Fitzwilliam Museum, Cambridge
Manchester and Birmingham showings only

Like *The Ladies' Lament* [cat. 24], this subject is from Scott's *Minstrelsy of the Scottish Border*. Taken from the eponymous ballad, it shows May Margaret kneeling on her alcove bed, raising a wand to her lips, as the ghost of her murdered lover Clerk Saunders enters through the wall, asking her to renew her vows.

The artist was first recorded at work on the subject in May 1854, when she designed a woodblock illustration (Ruskin Gallery 1991, 65) for a projected ballad book [see cat. 25]. Further studies are seen in the 1866 photographic record of Siddal's work (Fitzwilliam). Subject and treatment show the characteristically Pre-Raphaelite use of "medieval" subject matter to explore contemporary issues of class and gender. Like *Lady Clare* [cat. 23] and Keats' *Isabella*, painted by Millais in 1849 [fig.27, p.152], the story is one of love between social unequals. Objects in the room such as the prie-dieu suggest a medieval era and a female sphere of religious devotion.

Exhibited at the 1857 Russell Place show and included in the British Art exhibition sent to the USA later that year, *Clerk Saunders* was purchased by Charles Eliot Norton of Harvard. Bought back by Rossetti, it was later acquired by Charles Fairfax Murray, whose somewhat contentious inscription on the back begins, "This picture by Mrs Rossetti, esteemed by her husband the best of her works," and goes on to claim that, "Gabriel Rossetti himself worked on this picture as was customary with him, as Mr Burne-Jones told me long ago." But the work shows no distinct sign of Rossetti's hand; maybe Murray hoped to enhance its value by this statement, or confused it with *Sir Galahad at the Shrine* (1855-7, Tate Gallery 1984, no.217) which was signed by both artists.

### 26 Lady Affixing a Pennant to a Knight's Spear
c.1858/9
watercolour on paper
13.7 x 13.7
Tate Gallery.   Bequeathed by W.C. Alexander 1917

In this chivalric scene a medieval lady helps a knight fix a pennant to his lance, before he rides out to combat. Horse and squire wait at the castle door. The subject is imaginary or generic, as in comparable works of the same date by Rossetti (*Before the Battle*, MFA, Boston), Millais (*At the Tournament*, Ashmolean ), and Burne-Jones (*The Knight's Farewell*, Ashmolean [fig.20]), when the fashion for such intensely worked courtly subjects was at its height. All treatments derive ultimately from Maclise's *Spirit of Chivalry* (1845-7) for the Palace of Westminster, which was widely engraved. Siddal, however, chose to portray the business of chivalry in an almost domestic manner as, rather than embracing his lady, the knight struggles with hammer and nail. The subject may be compared with larger, later works by Bunce, *The Standard Bearer* [cat.71] and *The Keepsake* [cat.73] illustrating the long popularity of chivalric themes in Pre-Raphaelitism, though less generally favoured by female artists.

Compositionally, the work relates to Siddal's own *Lady Clare* [cat.23], with window and doorway leading to the outer world. The red of the pennon, symbolic of Love, unifyingly fills the space between the figures. Atmospherically, it is less enclosed, with a view of distant hills that may derive from the Peak District which Siddal visited in 1857/8. As

has been remarked, "[t]he contrast between the quiet, almost bare interior and the green landscape outside ... constructs again that opposition between the separate spheres of men and women." (Whitworth, 1984, no.45 ).

Owned by Philip Burne-Jones in 1904, the work was purchased for the Tate Gallery in 1912 and acquired in 1917. It bears a descriptive title of convenience, unlike most of Siddal's works which have literary or poetic titles.

# Rebecca Solomon

Born in London in 1832, the second of three children who all became artists, in a comfortably-off Jewish family. She was trained at the Spitalfields School of Design and advised by her elder brother Abraham, in whose studio she worked as an assistant and copyist until his death in 1862. Solomon worked as a copyist for other artists including William Frith and Millais: there is a replica of Millais' most famous work, *Christ in the House of his Parents* (1849-50) by her hand (priv. coll.). Her first exhibition in 1850 was as a copyist at the BI. During her career, she showed figure compositions in a range of topical genres usually in oil at RA, BI, SBA, SFA, Dudley, Birmingham, Liverpool, Glasgow, Leeds, French Gallery, Crystal Palace. She has been said to have suffered from alcoholism, but there is no documentary evidence for this claim. Sometimes accused of vulgarity in her subject-matter, she had her greatest success at the RA in 1860 with *Peg Woffington's Visit to Triplet* (unlocated). Abraham's death made her financial situation more precarious, and from 1863 she sought illustrative work while branching out also

into watercolour [see cat.27]. She was close to her younger brother Simeon at this time, as he too started to make a reputation as an artist. Travel on the Continent in the 1860s led to some Italianate subject-matter from 1867. Her last recorded exhibition was in 1874. She died in London in 1886 after being hit by a cab.

**27 The Wounded Dove**    1866
inscr monogram
watercolour on paper
47.5 x 37.5
The University of Wales, Aberystwyth College Collections

This drawing was exhibited at the British Institution and the Dudley Gallery in 1866, appearing the following year at the annual exhibition in Manchester and in 1868 in the annual Birmingham watercolour exhibition. Its subject seems to be of Solomon's own devising, though, as Elaine Shefer has demonstrated, the juxtaposition of a female figure with a bird in a domestic setting was quite a common idea by this time (Shefer, 1985). In its acknowledgement of burgeoning Aestheticism - a sumptuously dressed

woman of enigmatic mood, a touch of Japonisme - it follows up her *Primavera* (Bijuzha Inc., Tokyo) a watercolour shown at Dudley in 1865, in which the female figure, indeed, seems to be wearing the very same dress [fig.21].

It is probable, given the artistic acquaintance Solomon enjoyed, that she had noticed Burne-Jones's watercolour *Cinderella* (Boston Museum of Fine Arts) at the Old Watercolour Society's show in 1864, and Whistler's painting *Symphony in White no.2 (The Little White Girl)* (Tate Gallery) at the 1864 Academy, and borrowed from both these works to make *The Wounded Dove* fashionable. The influence of Whistler's picture is noticeable in precise details such as the mantelpiece, the dress and the model (in Whistler's painting, Jo Heffernan). Solomon became acquainted with Whistler as part of the circle that included her brother Simeon, who was also painting Japoniste pieces at this time, the neo-classical-cum-aesthetic

Fig.21
Rebecca Solomon, *Primavera*, 1864, Bijuzha Corporation, Japan

painter Albert Moore (with whom Simeon studied at the RA schools), the poet Algernon Swinburne and D.G. Rossetti.

This drawing was eventually sold to George Powell, a collector introduced to the Solomons by Swinburne. The correspondence between artist and patron shows the prosaically commercial character that the practice of art had for a single woman with no other means of support. "I trust you will pardon me for not having acknowledged before this the receipt of the ten pounds on account for the little picture ... I am much obliged to you for the remittance and shall be very glad to forward you the picture which you ought to have allowed me to do before this, and hope you are not waiting till you have settled for it, as I need not I am sure add it is not necessary, though I can assure you I shall find the balance most useful to me, as I am like too many others alas! much in want of the needful" (30th August 186?; University College of Wales, Aberystwyth). A letter of 1873 indicates that Solomon succeeded in selling further pictures to Powell, though no other work by her was in his collection when it was presented to the University College at Aberystwyth in 1882.

# Emma Sandys

Born 1843 in Norwich, the second child of Anthony Sands, a jobbing painter. Her brother Frederick, fourteen years her senior, also became an artist, in the Rossettian mould. She was taught by her father, though Fred - beginning to exhibit when she was still a child - became her chief advisor; common subjects, motifs and accessories are noticeable in their two oeuvres and her work has often been mistaken for his in the twentieth century [cat. 28]. Though her earliest surviving work is dated 1863, Sandys' exhibition debut was in 1867 with cat. 29. During her career, she exhibited portraits and female heads in oil supplemented by chalk drawings of the same subject matter, at RA, SLA, Norwich. She attracted many patrons from the Norwich region and, in two known instances, members of the aristocracy. She probably spent sporadic periods in her brother's London studio, but her address remained in Norwich throughout her career. Her last recorded exhibition was in 1874, though she continued to produce work until her death in November 1877 in Norwich of congestion of the lungs.

*Emma Sandys*, Reproduced by courtesy of the John Rylands University Library of Manchester

**28 Elaine** c.1862-5
oil on panel
38.3 x 40.7
The National Trust: Lanhydrock, Cornwall

Elaine is a heroine of Tennyson's *Idylls of the King* (1859) whose love for Lancelot is unrequited. A figure of pathos in the mid-Victorian imagination, the subject was often used by artists, especially women, e.g. Cameron (1874, RPS).

This painting is here attributed to Emma Sandys for the first time, on stylistic grounds. This would then be one of her earliest works. There are three known versions of this painting extant. One (priv. coll.) has been traditionally believed to be by the artist's brother Fred, tentatively identified as a portrait of the actress Ruth Herbert, and dated 1862-4 (Crombie). Another (priv. coll.), of similar dimensions and dated 1865, does bear Emma Sandys' monogram. The three works are identical but for a slight disparity in format. While the title painted on the frame is not necessarily original, a painting by Emma Sandys entitled *Elaine*, not currently identified, was exhibited in 1885 (no.102) at the Loan Exhibition for the Fund for the Restoration of St. Peter Mancroft Church at St. Andrew's Hall in Norwich. All three can be assumed to be the work of Emma rather than her brother, who is not recorded as having produced a work with the title *Elaine*.

A characteristic of Sandys' and her brother's joint oeuvres is the sharing and repetition of models, studio props and costumes. *Elaine* uses the leopard skin which lies on the floor in *Preparing for the Ball* [cat. 29] and can be discerned in the mirror of *Viola* [cat. 31], as well as a medievalising, decorative flat background that brings the figure forward found in numerous other works including *Lady in Yellow Dress* [cat. 30] and *Fiametta* (1876, Christie's 1993). The historical confusion over this work and its replicas is unsurprising. Fred also made replicas (there are over ten known versions of his *Proud Maisie*, c.1867-8: see Brighton Art Gallery and Museum) and Emma no doubt saw this as a way to increase her income.

### 29 Preparing for the Ball    1867
inscr monogram d.1867
oil on canvas
61 x 43
Private Collection

This painting has been identified as one of Sandys' two exhibits at the Norwich and Eastern Counties Working Classes Industrial Exhibition, in her home town of Norwich in 1867. The second painting was the currently unlocated *Girl with Butterfly*. This was apparently Sandys' first exhibition appearance, though her earliest known work dates from 1863 (*The Saxon Princess*, priv. coll.). It was no doubt in the nature of a 'trial run', since the following year saw Sandys' first appearance at a London venue when *Enid* (unlocated) was shown at the Academy.

The only full-length figure by Sandys currently known, *Preparing for the Ball,* hints at the success she might have had with this kind of picture despite what must be assumed to have been an informal training with her father and brother. In the event,

however, she specialised in half-lengths and busts such as cats. 30 and 31. This painting has attracted various titles since its recent reappearance at auction, including *Before the Mirror* and (the Pre-Raphaelite chestnut) Tennyson's *The Lady of Shalott*. A comparison with Lady Hawarden's contemporary photographs which pose her daughters in fanciful dress before a long mirror suggest the common currency of Sandys' composition, which she has nevertheless managed to infuse with movement and drama.

Though its provenance is unknown, a label on the back of this painting suggests it was exhibited at some time with the Yorkshire Fine Art and Industrial Institution, which held exhibitions in York from 1867.

### 30 Lady in Yellow Dress    c.1870
oil on panel
37 x 29.5
Norfolk Museums Service (Norwich Castle Museum)

This painting, whose exhibition record is unknown, bears all the hallmarks of Sandys' mature style and shows her attainment of the sophistication this genre evolved during the 1860s. The model is one of the artist's regulars, appearing in very different character in *Viola* [cat. 31]. The

work probably originally bore a literary or historical reference which is not currently known. The medievalising background uses a Flemish tapestry owned by the Norwich Castle Museum since 1861 also seen in the artist's *Olive* or *The Talking Oak* (1868, priv. coll.)

Interestingly, this idea was used in a female head (now lost) by the Sandys' friend, amateur artist Captain Roberts, which was noticed favourably by the local press at the first exhibition of the Norwich Fine Arts Association in 1868, at which Sandys also exhibited but with little critical success.

**31 Viola**   c.1870
oil on canvas
53 x 40.2
Board of Trustees of the National Museums & Galleries on Merseyside (Walker Art Gallery, Liverpool)

The frame bears the following lines from Shakespeare's *Twelfth Night*, Act II, Scene IV, "Duke: And what's her history? Viola: A blank, my Lord. She never told her love." This scene occurs when Viola, disguised as Cesario, banters with the Duke about love. The artist thus shows Viola not as she appears in the scene cited but as she is conjured by the dialogue, an unusual move in a subject frequently taken by painters. Viola was in the same league of popularity as Shakespeare's Ophelia, also treated by Sandys in a work presently unlocated, and Tennyson's *Mariana* [see cat. 48].

Though there is no doubt about the attribution of this work, which displays several of Sandys' characteristics such as the emphasis on the figure's jewels and costuming and the marmoreal jaw and hand, there are some curious aspects of the content that cast some doubt on its present identification. The motif of the closet is commonly found in contemporary depictions of the Arthurian character Enid, made familiar to the Victorians by Tennyson, and, indeed, there is no textual reference to a closet in the Shakespeare source quoted on the frame, rendering its significance in the present case indecipherable. (Sandys did exhibit an Enid at the Academy in 1868, currently unlocated). Further, the distant view outside the window makes more ready sense in relation to Enid, who was forced to leave her home and travel aimlessly through the land with her doubting husband Geraint, than to Viola. Another curious point about the content of this work under its present title is the room reflected in the mirror. Recalling the device in Brown's *Take Your Son, Sir!* (1856-7, Tate Gallery), it seems to show a Victorian rather than a medieval or Elizabethan interior.

Characteristic in many aspects of "second-wave" Pre-Raphaelitism, with its romantic medievalism, *Viola* was not apparently exhibited by the artist, so may be assumed to have been a commission. It was bequeathed to the present collection in 1908 from the collection of Professor George and Mrs Constance E. Warr, also the owners of work by Fred Sandys.

**32 Anna & Agnes Young**   1870
inscr monogram d 1870
pencil and coloured chalks on paper
48 x 38
Private Collection

The sitters have been identified by the present owner as the older daughters of William Young of Dulwich, a Scot working for Lloyds as an underwriter, and Frances Galbraith, his Australian wife. Public records suggest the children were aged 8 and 4 in 1870. Sandys may have painted their younger sister in her 1870 portrait *Violet* (priv. coll.).

Sandys attracted a considerable number of commissions for child portraits, both in oil and chalks, and was able to produce compelling character studies within this traditionally unrespected genre. *Beatrice Blanche Cloakes* (1871, Sotheby's 1982) and *Lady Winifred Herbert* (1870, priv. coll.) [fig. 14] are amongst her most convincing paintings, while the present work suggests in its lesser refinement the bread-and-butter nature of portraiture. The medievalised style of inscription and the floral detail seen here, perhaps used for a symbolic effect which the currently sketchy biography of the sitters renders impenetrable, are used by Fred Sandys in his comparable 1877 drawing, *Portrait of Philip Arthur Flower and Mary Isabel Flower* (Flower coll.)

*Our thanks to Richard Smith for assistance in compiling this entry*

**33 A Fashionable Lady** 1873
s & d 1873
coloured chalks on tinted paper
46 x 33.5
Private Collection

This elegant, lyrical drawing is as yet unidentified but represents an important aspect of Sandys's output. It bears no obvious identification with the works Sandys is known to have exhibited in and around 1873, so may well be a commissioned portrait. Its finely-judged mixture of decorativeness and realism lends itself to the *Art Journal's* comment on the artist's *Fair Rosamund*, shown at the Society of Lady Artists in 1874. "It is, in effect, a portrait-study in crayon, of unusual finish, and showing a careful studentship. The lines of the composition are firm, and so disposed as to indicate a deliberate and harmonious scheme; the expression upon the face is serious, and the general impression given by the work is of a fidelity in portraiture associated with artistic design" (*Art Journal*, 1 May 1874, 146).

The screen at the sitter's right shoulder is a sign of the Japonisme also seen in cats. 27 and 40.

# Julia Margaret Cameron
## *née* **Pattle**

H.H. Cameron,
*Portrait of J.M. Cameron*, 1870,
NMPFT/Science and Society Picture Library

Born in Calcutta in 1815, daughter of James Pattle of the East India Company and one of seven sisters famed for beauty and culture. In 1838 she married Charles H. Cameron, reforming jurist with the Supreme Council of India, where she spent the next ten years. In Britain with a growing family of six children, the Camerons eventually settled at Freshwater, Isle of Wight, near the Tennysons. Here she began photography in 1863, using an outdoor glasshouse and soon becoming a serious practitioner, joining professional bodies, entering competitions at home and abroad and contracting with art dealer Colnaghi for the sale of large-sized photographs, individually signed. Her innovative approach and prolific output made her a pioneer of art photography, a controversial field. According to her obituary, "her perfectly original photographic work ... after a daring fashion of her own, forfeit[ed] that sharpness of definition which ordinary photographers strive for, and which is one of the things artists most dislike in photographic portraiture, and having the advantage of sitters usually distinguished for intellectual gifts or personal graces, she produced a series of heads and groups quite unique in their suggestiveness" (*Times* 4 March 1879). In addition to portraits of renowned men and women of her day, including Tennyson, Carlyle, Darwin, Herschel and members of the PRB [cats.35,36], Cameron favoured subjects from scripture, history and literature in the manner of fine art [cats.37, 38]. Stylistically she allied herself with the Pre-Raphaelite school and the Italianate art of G.F. Watts. In a career lasting little more than a decade her pictures won prizes in Berlin and Paris and were shown in London exhibitions in 1866 and 1868. In 1874 Cameron began, at Tennyson's request, a major series of illustrations to his *Idylls of the King*, published in two parts in 1874/5. In 1875 her husband retired to Ceylon (now Sri Lanka) where Cameron continued photography with local models, and where she died in 1879.

## 34 Baby 'Pictet'    1864
s & inscr
albumen photographic print from wet collodian negative
17.2 x 14.7  (with arched top)
The National Museum of Photography, Film & Television (by courtesy of the Board of Trustees of the Science Museum)

According to the artist's inscription, the sitter is a "One year old Infant shipwrecked once in the Madras Surf & again in the wreck of the Colombo Steamer." The artist's niece Rose married Captain Francis Pictet of the 49th Madras Infantry, and this is presumed to be a portrait of their child, apparently perceived as a celebrity in her or his own right.

The steamship Colombo ran aground in the Indian Ocean in November 1862, so this startlingly direct portrait must come from early in Cameron's career. It presumably post-dates *Annie - My First Success* (January 1864, NPG) which shows a similar unadorned naturalism. If so, *Baby Pictet* would be aged about one and a half. Cameron began photography at the end of 1863, setting to work "alone & unassisted" in her converted glasshouse. "All thro' the severe month of January I felt my way literally in the dark thro' endless failures, at last came endless successes! May I not call them so?" she wrote in February (quoted Ford, 1975, 15). At the time, sitters had to keep motionless for extended periods and commercial photographers regarded babies as the most intractable subjects.

Here, a baby portrait is remarkable for the strong sense of individual character that emanates from the sitter and for its repudiation alike of the sentimentality and idealisation commonly found in traditional maternal imagery, both of which featured in Cameron's subsequent work, where babies are shown either as angels or in Madonna and Child poses. It may also be compared with Boyce's *Sidney Wells* [cat. 15] and intriguingly also with the Christ Child in Stokes's *Madonna* [cat.75] suggesting a distinctive quality of observation in female artists.

## 35 William Holman Hunt    1864
s & inscr 'W. Holman Hunt / in his Eastern dress / from life'
albumen photographic print from wet collodion negative
25.9 x 20.8
The National Museum of Photography, Film & Television (by courtesy of the Board of Trustees of the Science Museum)

Founder member of the PRB, W. Holman Hunt (1827-1910) was the most faithful to its original ideals. His travels to Egypt and Palestine in pursuit of authentic backgrounds for Biblical subjects and the 1860 exhibition of his *The Finding of the Saviour in the Temple* (Birmingham Museum and Art Gallery) made him a prime candidate for Cameron's "hall of fame" - large-scale portraits of leading men. At the time of this portrait his prestigious picture, *London Bridge on the Night of the Marriage of the Prince and Princess of Wales* (1864, Ashmolean) was on show at the New Gallery.

The sitting for this portrait, one of several, took place in May 1864, at the Hendon home of her sister Maria Jackson, also a friend of the painter, who here wears the Middle Eastern costume in which he often chose to be portrayed. When one portrait from this session was shown the same month at the Photographic Society exhibition, Hunt told F.G. Stephens he "really regarded it as a very flattering represent-ation of myself ... my impression certainly was that it made my face less ugly than I was accustomed to see it in the glass." He was sorry it was not better liked, "principally on account of Mrs Cameron whose purse I hoped it might help to fill." (Bodleian). He added that as the photographer herself was dissatisfied with most of those taken, he would offer another sitting, which took place in 1865.

The work demonstrates Cameron's ambition at the start of her career, comparing in its presentation of a heroic-romantic figure with G.F. Watts's sequence of "men of the time" begun in 1856 (NPG). Other sitters selected from the PRB circle include William Rossetti [cat.36] and Thomas Woolner [fig. 12]. Like fellow artist Watts and fellow photographer C.L. Dodgson (Lewis Carroll) she sought out celebrities, transforming the "penny portraits" of the famous sold by the thousand into more serious artistic works. Her stated object in male portraiture was to go beyond mere likeness. "When I have such men before my camera, my whole soul has endeavoured to do its duty towards them in recording faithfully the inner as well as the outer man," she wrote in *Annals of my Glass House* (quoted Hopkinson, 12). Though Hunt's work was not a notable Pre-Raphaelite influence on Cameron, this image shows a convincing understanding of his character. Her sequence of portraits showing him in Arab dress has been described as a "collaborative effort towards defining Hunt as an Orientalist" in an age when exploration and trade were bringing "the East" under European political and economic influence (Lori Cavagnaro, in Oliphant, 128-131).

*Our thanks to Judith Bronkhurst for assistance in compiling this entry.*

### 36 William Michael Rossetti    1865
albumen photographic print from wet collodion negative
25.3  x 20.3
National Portrait Gallery, London

William M. Rossetti (1829-1919) was a member of the PRB and brother to the more famous Dante Gabriel. Known chiefly as a critic, here he is portrayed as the artist he half aspired to be. Hitherto ascribed to 1866, this is one of two images of the sitter exhibited at Colnaghi's at the end of 1865 in Cameron's first solo show (reviewed in *Macmillan's Magazine*, January 1866.).

W.M. Rossetti admired "our good old friend, the enthusiastic Mrs Cameron" and in May 1865 had urged F.G. Stephens to notice her work at the Photographic Society, saying "[N]o doubt you know her photographs and their exceptional artistic value." (Peattie). Stephens' review

compared her compositions to "those of Della Robbia, in their suavity and intelligent expressiveness," and particularly commended her portraits of Tennyson and Watts (*Athenaeum* 20 May 1865, 690).

Later that year the artist invited Rossetti to Little Holland House, Kensington, to sit for his portrait at the same time as Robert Browning, shown similarly draped (Weaver 3.14). According to the artist, she had "never print[ed] out the hand holding the umbrella because I always remember too vividly it is B r o w n i n g ' s hand!!" (UT) but the poet's knuckles are clearly visible on the far right of  the image. Cameron's practice was to make full-size prints from negatives, without cropping or re-touching.

Afterwards, she was disappointed at the lack of response. "My dear Mr Rossetti", she wrote in January 1866, "I have never heard from you and only once of you since the afternoon when you very devotedly did your best for me & I in my turn did my best with you. For I verily believe I have never had more remarkable success with any Photograph but I should like to know if you yourself are of this opinion, for I have never heard even whether you approved of the picture!" She hoped he would visit Colnaghi's and also give his opinion publicly, to promote sales. "Have you no means of introducing any friendly Paragraphs into any Paper that had good circulation. I myself delight in both those Pictures of you - yet if you judge any differently I would not have you otherwise than quite candid with me." (UT).

**37 Group from Browning's 'Sordello'**   1867
s & inscr 'group from Sordello by Browning'
28.9 x 23.4
albumen photographic print from wet collodian negative
The National Museum of Photography, Film & Television (by courtesy of the Board of Trustees of the Science Museum)

Published in 1840, Sordello is a complex narrative poem by Robert Browning, telling the tale of the eponymous Italian "knight, bard and gallant" in six books. Regarded as too dense and difficult by most readers, it was popular with the Pre-Raphaelite Brothers. For her well-constructed figure group composition, Cameron has chosen a romantic moment from Book II, when Sordello wins a troubadour contest and is rewarded by Palma, his beloved:

> She lent, speaking some six words and no more.
> He answered something, anything; and she
> Unbound a scarf and laid it heavily
> Upon him, her neck's warmth and all...

The sitters were Henry Cotton, a young gentleman, and Mary Ryan, Cameron's parlourmaid and frequent model. The romantic subject had personal import, for the sitting took place a few days before the wedding of Cotton and Ryan on the Isle of Wight, with Cameron and her husband as witnesses.

Cameron's aim was, "to enable Photography and secure for it the character and uses of High Art by combining the real and Ideal and sacrificing nothing of Truth by all possible devotion to Poetry and beauty." (Ford, 140). Pictorially a most successful narrative subject, her Sordello may be compared to Lucy Brown's images of young lovers [cats.40 and 41]. With Siddal's Pippa Passes [cat.20] and Brickdale's I did no more... [cat.84] the subject testifies to the popularity of Browning's work with all Pre-Raphaelite generations.

**38 Hypatia**   1868
s & inscr 'from life / Freshwater 1868' with title.
albumen photographic print from wet collodian negative
32.5 x 25.5
Private Collection

Hypatia, neo-Platonist scholar, was torn to death in AD 415 under the fanatical St. Cyril of Alexandria. Her story was re-told in Charles Kingsley's controversial novel Hypatia (1853), the text to which Cameron linked her representation, choosing however to portray Hypatia in Renaissance costume. Weaver, who describes Cameron's pictorial images as "an

idealization of vital womanhood from the living model" draws attention to the bridging of eras, calling Hypatia "an intellectual martyr between two dispensations, the classical and the Christian." (91-2). In 1865 Solomon exhibited (Dudley Gallery) a watercolour Hypatia, using a classical figure for "a picture which might otherwise have stood for a portrait of one of Tennyson's learned women" (Spectator 4 March 1865, 243), suggesting that the subject was well recognised at this date.

The model was fellow artist Marie Spartali, aged 25 in September 1868. She also sat for Cameron for the Imperial Eleanore and Mnemosyne, mother of the Muses. Using the same model for several ideal types was a technique deployed by Rossetti from 1868 onwards. Admiring Rossetti's work, in 1867 Cameron presented him with seven photographs, mainly the female heads of her middle period. The half-length framing of Hypatia recalls his "Venetian" image Monna Vanna of 1866 [fig.22] who also has a fan and sumptuous sleeves. The gown with its loops of ribbon was the sitter's own, and this photograph is among those presented by the artist to her sitter.

Fig.22
D.G. Rossetti,
Monna Vanna, 1866,
Tate Gallery

The depiction of an historical figure links up with Cameron's Sappho (1865, V&A) and Boadicea (NPG) as a sequence of "famous women" in a manner much favoured in the Victorian era. The choice of subjects from an artist not usually associated with feminism connects her to

Bodichon and Boyce, whose *Elgiva* [cat.14] is a comparable figure. Charles Mitchell's later, highly sensational image of a naked *Hypatia* (RA 1885, Laing) underlines the beauty and dignity of Cameron's interpretation.

**39 Zuleika**  c. 1864-7
replica print
33.5 x 25.2 (arched top)
Wellcome Institute Library, London

Zuleika is the tragic heroine of Byron's narrative poem *The Bride of Abydos* (1815), victim of the conflict between romantic love and a politically arranged marriage. Popular during Cameron's youth, the poem sensationalises 'Oriental despotism' and dramatises the divided loyalties of a loving daughter who responds to the desires of her heart. The lines that most nearly correspond to the image are those in which Selim watches Zuleika through a lattice door:

> She snatched the urn wherein was mixed
> The Persian Atar-gul's perfume,
> And sprinkled all its odours o'er
> The pictured roof and marble floor.

As yet insecurely dated, the image is linked by Weaver (3,51) to that of Rebecca, traditionally shown with a pitcher. But *Zuleika* is also one of several renderings of female figures in "Eastern" dress such as *Pharaoh's Daughter* (1866, RPS) and *Woman in Egyptian Costume* (c. 1873, UT) which indicate Cameron's range of pictorial invention. It may be compared with Holman Hunt's full-length figure *The Afterglow in Egypt* (1863, Southampton). While it would be nice to see in her choice of Byron's doomed heroine a contemporary comment on the subjection of women, it is more likely that Cameron was attracted to the Romantic aspect of Zuleika's story.

Based on her practice when focusing of stopping when "coming to something which to my eye was very beautiful" (P.H.Emerson, *Sun Artists*, 1891), Cameron's much-discussed soft-focus treatment reflects her idealising conception in the manner of High Art to which she aspired in her chosen art form. It reminds us that G.F. Watts and D.G. Rossetti were Cameron's favourite artists, who in turn admired her works as "the only photography in the world that gives them pure, unmixed delight." (Gernshein, 1975, 46).

# Lucy Madox Brown
## *later* Rossetti

*Lucy Madox Brown,* 1866, Delaware Art Museum, Helen Farr Sloan Library Archives

Born in Paris July 1843, the eldest of Ford Madox Brown's three surviving children and only child of his first marriage. After her mother's death in 1846, her father returned to Britain and Lucy lived with her aunt in Gravesend until on re-marriage he was able to provide a home for her. From an early age she acted as her father's model, secretary and studio assistant, but began painting herself only in 1868, under his guidance. Her first exhibition was at the RA in 1869 (*Painting,* untraced). During her career, she appeared, largely as watercolourist with figure compositions drawn from modern life, literature and history [cats. 40, 41, 43], at RA, Dudley, Birmingham, Manchester, Liverpool. She visited Belgium and Germany with William and Jane Morris in 1869 and Italy in 1873 with the Bell Scotts, Alice Boyd and W.M. Rossetti. In 1874 she married William Rossetti, fourteen years her senior, returning to Italy on honeymoon. Her first child was born in 1875, second in 1877, third in 1879, and twins in 1881 (one dying in infancy). After becoming a mother, she painted little and from 1885 showed signs of respiratory disease, which obliged her to leave London periodically for healthier locations such as Isle of Wight (January-May 1886) and Italian Riviera (January-March 1887). Radical in her political and cultural interests, she was a signatory of the 1889 national petition for women's suffrage and published a biography of Mary Shelley in the series *Eminent Women*, 1890. She also wrote an unpublished biography of her father, who died in 1893. She left England for Italy on account of her health in the autumn of 1893 and died in San Remo in April 1894. The large watercolour *Romeo and Juliet* (1871, on loan to Wightwick Manor), said by many contemporaries to be her best work, was included in Masterpieces of English Art, 1896.

**40 The Duet**   1870
s & d  'LMB - 70'
watercolour on paper
57.1 x 42.5
Private Collection

This "young lovers" scene bears a double meaning, as a romantic as well as musical duet. On the spinet is an image of Orpheus taming the beasts with his lyre. At the RA in 1870 the work was unjustly "skied" but received commendation for its, "great spirit, rich tones and fine colouring" (*Athenaeum*, 747). Its period charm contrasts with the contemporaneity of *Après le Bal* (priv. coll.), the artist's other large watercolour shown this year (Dudley Gallery).

Stylistically, *The Duet* reflects both Brown's debt to her father and her own individuality. The cropping of the male figure is suggestive of avant-garde effects in French art of this period, while the screen (which appears in F.M. Brown's 1877 self-portrait) builds an unexpected range of references into a distinctive treatment that combines contemporaneity, japonisme, Regency revival and Rossettianism. According to the artist, the accessories were chosen for their tastefulness and appropriateness to the period chosen (Clayton, 119-20). The identity of the models is not recorded, but it is likely that the artist's musically gifted sister Cathy sat for the woman.

According to surviving correspondence, the work was purchased for 50gns. in July 1870 by F.W. Craven of Manchester, who, as was his custom, requested various alterations. The artist's father, replying on her behalf on 24 August, observed that the features and expression had "always been much admired & the position of the little finger has much to do with the look of playing in reality, as opposed to a listless way of merely placing a hand on the keys. However both shall be well considered before you get the work back again." (UT) Although Craven had already paid he reneged on the purchase, and in 1871 the work went to Liverpool priced at 60 gns. It appeared again at the Dudley in 1877 and subsequently remained in the family.

Praised by D.G. Rossetti as "a really perfect picture," *The Duet* was also described as imbued with the spirit of his "school" although painted with a more exquisite touch (*Magazine of Art*, 1870, 342). To Percy Bate, with *Romeo & Juliet* it exemplified Brown's attributes, being tender, "full of thought, full of the very soul of the artist; and ...[with] an added charm beyond the beauty of presentation or the poetry of colour." (Bate, 22 ) Similar double meanings were popular in the Aesthetic works of Albert Moore, Rossetti and Burne-Jones, as well as Frank Dicksee (*Harmony*, 1877, Tate).

**41 Ferdinand and Miranda Playing Chess**   1871
s & d  'LMB - 71'
oil on canvas
68.6 x 61
Private Collection

The scene here is from *The Tempest*, Act V, when Prospero's cave opens to reveal "Ferdinand and Miranda, playing at chess":

Mir.   Sweet lord, you play me false.
Fer.             No, my dearest love,
I would not for the world.
Mir.   Yes, for a score of kingdoms you should wrangle,
And I would call it fair play.

Ferdinand's father Alonso, seeing the son he thought drowned, fears it yet another "vision of the island".

This is Lucy Brown's first exhibited work in oils and builds on the success of *Romeo at the Tomb of Juliet* (1871). Both recall early Pre-Raphaelite fondness for Shakespearean scenes such as *King Lear* by the artist's father (1849, Tate Gallery) or Millais' *Ferdinand lured by Ariel* (1849-50, Tate Gallery 1984, no.24). A scene from *The Tempest* was depicted in photography by Cameron in 1865. Together with *The Magic Mirror* (priv. coll.), a large watercolour the subject of which is taken from Spenser, *Ferdinand and Miranda* was sent in 1872 to the Dudley Gallery and then to Liverpool, priced at 80 gns.

The artist's sister Cathy, her most frequent model, sat for the figure of Miranda, and William Rossetti, whom the artist would marry in 1874, for that of Prospero. Ferdinand was drawn from the artist's brother Oliver, who in his own short career as an artist produced a picture of Prospero and Miranda being shipwrecked, exhibited in 1871.

Both subject and treatment suggest an ambition to live up to the view of the "uncommon power [which] warrants high expectations of the young artist's future." (*Times* 11 February. 1871, 4).

## 42 Mathilde Blind  1872
s & d 'LMB - 72'
black, red and white chalks on grey paper
77 x 55
Lent by the Principal and Fellows of Newnham College, Cambridge

Mathilde Blind (1841-1896) was a German-born poet and feminist, whose step-father Karl Blind was involved in the 1848 revolution and later moved to Britain, where the Blinds became close friends of the Browns. Her brother committed suicide when arrested after attempting to assassinate Bismarck in 1866. She held radical political views and revered a pantheon of women - George Sand, George Eliot and Elizabeth Barrett Browning. Asked what men could do when women took over the professions, she replied, "Emigrate" (Kaplan, 161).

Drawn when the sitter was 32 and the artist 29, this portrait of one idealistic young woman by another antedates that of the same sitter by F.M. Brown. Despite a rather academic use of its medium it succeeds in conveying a woman of determination and spirit. According to the artist's husband W.M. Rossetti, who met Blind in 1869, she was, "of Jewish race, with a fine, animated, speaking countenance, and an ample stock of interesting and pointed conversation," (Rossetti, W.M., 1906, ii, 388). Both artist and sitter wrote for the *Eminent Women* series. Inheriting a fortune in middle life, Blind left money to the artist's impoverished sister and the bulk of her estate to Newnham College, Cambridge, for the advancement of women's education.

In 1906 the portrait was owned by Blind's friends Mr & Mrs Alfred Mond, who invited the artist's widower to see it. "I found that Mrs M[ond] considered it to be very little of a likeness of Mathilde Blind, and she says the same of the head done by Madox Brown," he reported. "I told her expressly however that I consider them both to be correct likeness, according to their several dates." In characteristically tepid manner, he continued, "The question was raised as to what might be a fair price to put upon the head by Lucy. It is an approvable work of art, without being a remarkably good one. Of course heads done in tinted chalks do not, as such, command very high prices. I think that the portrait is quite reasonably worth £22 to 25, but would not rate it at a higher figure than this." (UT). It was presented to the College in 1929 by Helen Chamberlain Beesley, former Newnham student, who presumably received it from the Monds.

## 43 Margaret Roper Rescuing the Head of her Father Sir Thomas More  1873
s & d 'LMB - 1873'
oil on canvas
63 x 49
Lent anonymously

A label on the back of this dramatic history painting describes the scene portrayed: "Margaret Roper by night stealthily removes the head of her father Sir Thomas More from London Bridge, A.D. 1534". Lord Chancellor More was executed for refusing to support Henry VIII's divorce and so in accord with custom, his severed head was placed on a spike at the entrance to London Bridge. His daughter Margaret removed it for reverent burial, an act of courage and filial honour that, together with her reputation for learning, elevated her into the histories of "famous women" popular in the 19th century as female role models.

The subject, therefore, is heroic and English, and as such may be compared with Boyce's *Elgiva* [cat. 14] and Howitt's lost *Boadicea*. The choice of incident moves away from standard Victorian representations, such as J.R. Herbert's motionless depiction of *Roper Visiting More in the Tower* (RA, 1844), and other treatments by Hart (RA, 1845) and Yeames (RA 1863). Among the most ambitious of the artist's works, it reflects the characteristic Madox Brown liking for high drama, as in F.M. Brown's *Haidee Finding Don Juan* (1878), while also recalling Millais's modern-day *Rescue* of 1855 (Melbourne). The challenging perspective and somewhat loose handling demonstrate a development from the relatively static *Ferdinand and Miranda*, while the night-time river view behind shows certain affinities with Whistler's Thames-side nocturnes. It is possible that the model for Roper was Mathilde Blind [cat. 42]

First exhibited at Liverpool in 1873, *Margaret Roper* was seen at the Dudley Gallery in 1875 (price 120 gns) and at Manchester in the same year (£250). The high prices indicate the artist's estimate of its merits, though buyers probably found the subject ill-suited to a domestic setting. The work was presented to a church by the artist's grand-daughter.

**44 Portrait of André**     c.1889
chalks on coloured paper
56 x 45.8
Private Collection
Manchester showing only

"She had done some very superior work in point of invention, expression and colouring and was steadily advancing in general execution and handling", wrote the artist's widower in 1906. "She was ambitious of excelling and not indifferent to fame; and she had an exalted idea of art and its potencies. After our marriage [in 1874] she tried more than once to set resolutely to work again; but the cares of a growing family, delicate health and the thousand constant interruptions which are not the less real at the time for being dim in the after-memory always impeded her, and very much to her disappointment and vexation she did not succeed in producing any more work adapted for exhibition." (Rossetti, W.M., 1906, ii, 432).

One "care" to which the artist devoted herself was her children's education. She also for a while housed their three cousins, after the death of their father [see cat. 45]. The youngest of these was Juliet, who later recalled the son of a cook in the household who complained of having to wear a page-boy's jacket and answer the door. Proclaiming himself a "son of France", he told the other children that in his homeland the people had executed all tyrants (Soskice, 2). It seems likely that the present work is a portrait of this boy, whom family tradition names André. If so, it probably dates from around 1888-90. Evidently later than the portrait of Mathilde Blind [cat. 42], it is considerably looser in handling, showing a marked development in fluency and rhythm.

# Catherine Madox Brown
*later* **Hueffer**

Born 1850, the first child of Ford Madox Brown's second marriage to Emma Hill, and second of his three surviving children. Her earliest memories were of modelling for her father as a babe in arms, and of visits by the Rossetti brothers. She attended Queen's College, the girls' school in Harley St. and was trained in art by her father, with whom she also worked as model and studio assistant. Her first exhibition was at the RA in 1869 (*At the Opera*, priv. coll). She subsequently appeared chiefly as a watercolourist with fancy pictures (e.g. *M'liss* 1874, untraced, and *A Deep Problem*, see Clayton, 1876, ii, 96) and portraits at RA, Dudley, Manchester, Liverpool. In 1872, she married Franz Hueffer, German musicologist, spending the honeymoon in France and Italy. Her children were born in 1873, 1877 and 1881, her firstborn becoming the writer Ford Madox Ford. Her husband's death in 1889 left her in financial straits; she was refused a Civil List pension. Though she is generally thought to have ceased painting in the mid-1870s, there is evidence [cat. 47] to indicate that she attempted to resume her career in the 1890s. Her last recorded exhibition was in 1901. She died in 1927.

F.M. Brown,
*Portrait of Catherine Madox Brown with Colour Box, c.* 1870,
Private Collection

**45 Ford Madox Brown at the Easel** 1870
s & d 'CMB - 70'
watercolour on paper
53.5 x 48.2
Private Collection

In 1870 the artist completed portraits of each parent. This shows her father Ford Madox Brown (1821 - 1893), a close and early associate of the PRB. Like his own *The Nosegay* (186l, Walker Art Gallery) for which the artist sat, the setting, with its typical brick wall between properties, was presumably the back garden of the family home in Fitzroy Square. The view, however, is almost identical to that in his *Stages of Cruelty* (1856-90, Manchester City Art Galleries, [fig.23]) for which she also sat, as a child, and which was painted at the former family home in Kentish Town. Some conscious homage may thus be intended, in addition to the tribute to her father's profession conveyed by showing him in characteristic pose at the easel. Though the subject of his canvas here can only be conjectured, this can be construed as a quasi-reciprocal image, and testifies to shared artistic endeavour. Just as she shows him with a palette, a portrait drawing of Cathy by her father done at around the same date shows her with an open colour-box (priv. coll.).

The companion full-length portrait of the artist's mother Emma Hill Brown, entitled *Thinking*, [fig.16, Phillips 4 November 1985, 191] was praised for colour, expression and tone (*Athenaeum*, 1870, 747). The sitters are in complementary settings - mother indoors sewing, father outdoors painting. Though not identical in size, they seem to have been conceived as a pair. As *Thinking* was sent to the RA, it may be that the present work was not finished in time for submission. It was exhibited in Liverpool in 1872 and included in the International Exhibition at South Kensington the same year. It appears not to have been offered for sale and remains in the family, as does a preliminary study.

The mood of the picture is tenderly melancholy, suggesting

Fig.23
F.M. Brown,
*Stages of Cruelty*, 1856-90, Manchester City Art Gallery

the artist understood her father's inner as well as outer personality. Its handling clearly reveals her debt to his training. Portraits of the same sitter exist by Rossetti (1852, NPG) and Millais (1853, Ashmolean) as well as his self portrait of 1877 (Harvard).

**46 Francis Hueffer, the Artist's Husband** 1873
watercolour on paper
78.8 x 61
Private Collection

Franz Hüffer (1845-1889), whom the artist married in 1872, was born in Germany and anglicised his name on settling in Britain, where in 1879 he became music critic on the *Times*. From a prosperous publishing family in Westphalia, he was known among the Pre-Raphaelites as a passionate admirer of Schopenhauer and Wagner. He also published a book on the Troubadour poets (1878) and edited D.G. Rossetti's poems for Tauchnitz. He died suddenly, leaving his wife with three children and very little money.

Christina Rossetti described Hueffer as "a learned German", appropriately young for his bride. William Rossetti remembered him as a "rather bulky man, of very Teutonic physiognomy, brilliant yellow hair [and] blue eyes radiant with quickness and penetration." (Rossetti, W.M., 1906, 332). In his wife's image he appears slighter, but the eyes are indeed penetrating.

The portrait, here exhibited for the first time, was originally in a larger frame. It is likely to have been drawn in mid-1873 as by April, when she sent to the RA a well-received portrait of fellow-artist Laura Alma-Tadema, the artist was pregnant with her first child. The half-length of her husband offers a sensitive rendering of the male image, with stylistic similarities to the work of her father, as for example his 1864 portrait of James Leathart (priv. coll.) It demonstrates her talent for taking a likeness and feeling for domestic portraiture.

Together with cat. 45 and cat. 47, the three sitters depicted by the artist represent three family generations, taken from figures close at hand both literally and emotionally. They thus demonstrate the concerns and the constraints of the female artist, and contrast with Cameron's wider range.

**47 Elsie Martindale Hueffer**     1895
s & d 'CMFH 95' and inscribed 'Elsie Madox Hueffer'
pastel and pencil on paper
63.5 x 53.5
Private Collection

Elsie Martindale (1876-1949) married Ford Hueffer in 1894 and thus became the artist's daughter-in-law. Despite the inscription, Madox was never part of her name. Opposed by the Martindales, the marriage was encouraged by the artist, who doted on her elder son. At the time of

her engagement, the sitter was described as "exceedingly pretty & not merely so, but she has a soul in her face with gold threads in her brown hair, the oval sweep from ear to chin, and a light deep down in her hazel eyes, especially the light in her eyes. At times she smiled in their depths as at a secret happiness. She has too, charming manners & neither conceit nor shyness" (Johnson, 1989, 162).

At the time of painting the artist was living in Chiswick, west London, where she shared a painting room with her second son Oliver. Finished around March 1895, the portrait was shown to Olive Garnett, who wrote: "It is a regular Madox Brown, very like Elsie (in her green dress & large black hat) & very artistic, thoroughly characteristic of painter and model ... A wedding ring is also conspicuous & the family have therefore dubbed it 'Portrait of a wedding ring'" (Johnson, 1993, 159).

The artist was dismayed when painter Frederic Shields "found a great many faults" in her picture. She also complained of never being left in peace to paint and though at this date she seems to have wished to resume her career, hindrances continued and the present work is the latest known. Its assured treatment shows she had not lost her touch since her last appearance in public (1875, Manchester City Art Galleries). Never before exhibited, the work has been passed down via the sitter's daughter and grand-daughter, who are of course also descended from the artist.

# Marie Spartali
## *later* Stillman

Born in Middlesex in 1843, daughter of Michael Spartali, import-export merchant and sometime Greek consul in London, and by birth and acquaintance like Zambaco a member of the cultured Greek community in London whose doyen was Constantine Ionides. Trained under Ford Madox Brown from 1864-70, alongside his daughters, Spartali was also friend to Burne-Jones, and occasional model for Brown, Rossetti and Cameron [cat. 38]. Her earliest exhibited works such as *The Lady Prays - Desire* (Dudley, 1867) and *Antigone* (Dudley, 1871, priv. coll.) show consciously feminist and political themes linked to her own experience and heritage. In 1871 she married against her family's wish the American

Lisa Stillman, *Portrait of Marie Spartali Stillman*, unlocated, photograph courtesy of the British Library

journalist and amateur artist W.J. Stillman; they had three children, one of whom died in infancy. Owing to her husband's work as newspaper correspondent the family settled in Florence in 1878, and then Rome until 1898. Despite prolonged residences abroad, Spartali became a regular contributor to Grosvenor Gallery 1877-87 and its successor the New Gallery as well as at various venues in eastern USA. Her sustained output proves her professionalism, but little of her work seems to have sold. Her favoured subjects were literary-historical figure groups and decorative female heads preferred by patrons; landscapes and flower pieces are equally representative though less distinctive. Many of her works draw on Italian literary themes, especially Dante and Boccaccio [see cats. 51, 52] as well as depicting Italian landscape. Her daughter Euphrosyne (Effie) became an artist, as did her step-daughter Lisa Stillman; her son Michael was an architect and settled in America, where retrospective shows were held in 1908 and 1982. She died in Britain in 1927.

**48 Mariana**  c. 1867-9
watercolour on paper
38 x 27.5
Private Collection

The figure of Mariana comes from Shakespeare's *Measure for Measure* via Tennyson's poem *Mariana*, a quotation from which is inscribed on the back, "Alas she said my life is dreary / He cometh not." Confined to a moated grange, Mariana vainly awaits the arrival of her lover.

This drawing, an undocumented work, belongs with early pieces such as the artist's exhibition debut *The Lady Prays - Desire* (1867, private collection) and *Forgetfulness* (1869, Sotheby's 1969). Produced during or soon after her training with F.M. Brown, the name and address on the label indicate that it certainly dates from before her marriage.

Fig. 24
Marie Spartali Stillman,
*Love's Messenger,*
Delaware Art Museum

The medieval setting and costume begin a trend in her oeuvre to which she remained faithful, growing in conviction and sophistication through such works as *Love's Messenger* (c.1885, Delaware [fig.24]) and *Beatrice* (1895-6, Delaware). Of the former, Spartali wrote that the composition was suggested by, "the effect of a fair head in a certain bull's eye window of a friend's studio where I was working one winter." (Delaware, 174). Though it is not known whose studio this refers to, "round glass" panes were installed by Morris & Co in Burne-Jones's house in Fulham around 1868-70.

Millais's arresting *Mariana* (1851, Makins Collection), with the same quotation, became the paradigm for a theme chosen regularly by artists within and beyond Pre-Raphaelitism (including Bunce with an unlocated work of 1891). Her taste formed rather by Brown's earnestness than Millais's liking for sentiment, Spartali conventionally depicts the heroine as a forlorn victim of male caprice, an image of unfulfilled love like Sandys' *Viola* [cat.31]. The mood, however, is not so maudlin as to render the motive definitive; without the title Mariana appears a pensive figure, redolent of Blunden's seamstress [cat.11] as much as of Tennyson's weary captive.

Though the label attached to this work suggests it was sent for exhibition, no record has yet been traced.

**49 Self Portrait**  1871
s & d with monogram and '71'
charcoal and white chalk on paper board
63.5 x 51.5
Delaware Art Museum. Gift of Lucia N. Valentine

Drawn around the time of her marriage, this is a serious yet somewhat romanticised portrayal of the artist as a pensive, elegant Renaissance lady, at a Titianesque ledge. The historicised staging and suave treatment suggest it was also an exercise in the bust-length portraits that Rossetti and Fred Sandys made such a commercial success in chalks and pencil (e.g. Rossetti's *Aglaia Coronio*, 1870, V&A, and Sandys' *Mary Sandys*, c.1873, Birmingham Museum and Art Gallery).

The design, which may be compared with Cameron's rendering of Spartali as *Hypatia* [cat.38], was evidently made in more than one version. Henry James described a very similar watercolour exhibited in 1874 in the United States (unlocated). "The picture represents a lady (the artist herself, we believe) leaning on the parapet of a balcony, with one arm lying along the stone work and the left hand holding up, near her cheek, a half-opened fan. She is extremely beautiful; she is dressed in a picturesque robe of sombre red, cut low and square upon the bosom, and behind her are seen a few green branches from a plant in a tub," he wrote, adding that the picture contained no bright colour and its interest resided chiefly "in the remarkable, the almost touching, good faith of the work. The type of face and the treatment suggest the English pre-Raphaelite school, but in so far as the artist is a pre-Raphaelite, she is evidently a sincere and, as we may say, a natural one ... its patience, its refinement, its deep pictorial sentiment, give the whole production a singular intensity " (*Atlantic Monthly*, January 1875, 119).

The present work was given by the artist to Wendell P. Garrison, probably after 1900.

## 50 Madonna Pietra degli Scrovigni 1884

s & d in monogram 1884
watercolour, gouache and gum arabic on paper
78.5 x 61.1
Board of Trustees of the National Museums &
Galleries on Merseyside (Walker Art Gallery,
Liverpool)

This drawing, based on poems by Dante, was exhibited at the Grosvenor Gallery and Liverpool Autumn Exhibition in 1884. "You will find a translation and notes on Dante's poem of Madonna Pietra degli Scrovigni in D.G. Rossetti's "Early Italian Poets", wrote the artist to E. Rimbault Dibdin, adding with characteristic diffidence, "[i]t is just a lady clad in green in a green stony landscape which repeats her name [pietra = stone]." (9 September 1884, Walker Art Gallery). The verse visualised here is from a sestina celebrating a woman identified by Rossetti as from Padua, home of the Scrovegni family, builders of the Arena Chapel (D.G. Rossetti, 1861, 324-7):

> Utterly frozen is this youthful lady
> Even as the snow that lies within the shade;
> ...
> A while ago I saw her dress'd in green,
> So fair, she might have waken'd in a stone
> This love which I do feel even for her shade.
> And therefore as one woos a graceful lady
> I wooed her in a field that was all grass,
> Girdled about with very lofty hills.

In 1874, Rossetti himself produced a nude *Madonna Pietra* in pastel (Surtees 1971 no.237) also holding a crystal sphere. In creating a far chaster image, Spartali has emphasised the winter-flowering blossoms of blackthorn and hellebore, given a Leonardesque cast to the frosty landscape, and characterised the Paduan beauty as a gentle rather than sensual figure. Within her glass sphere appears an Annunciation image, which may be the artist's suggestion that the stony-hearted lady places religious faith above courtly love-games.

In the early 1880s, Spartali had been resident for some years in Florence, with summer visits to the Italian Tyrol or Dolomites. Annually she sent or brought work for exhibition in Britain and was staying in Scotland when this drawing was bought on its appearance in Liverpool and presented to the Walker Art Gallery by Harold Rathbone on behalf of the subscribers.

## 51 Dante at Verona 1888

s & d in monogram '1888'
gouache and watercolour on paper
49.5 x 73.5
Private Collection

Exhibited at the New Gallery in 1888 (no.233), this was accompanied by a quotation from Rossetti's poem of the same name:

> he comes upon
> The women at their palm-playing.
> The conduits round the gardens sing
> And meet in scoops of milk-white stone,
> Where wearied damsels rest and hold
> Their hands in the wet spurt of gold.
> One of whom, knowing well that he,
> By some found stern, was mild with them,
> Would run and pluck his garment's hem,
> Saying, "Messer Dante, pardon me",
> Praying that they might hear the song
> Which first of all he made, when young.

The song Dante made "when young" is the *Vita Nuova*, which induces a pensive mood in both poet and listeners. The scene is an imagined re-creation of a public garden in medieval Verona, to which Dante was exiled, with fountains, orange-trees, and background city-scape derived either from observation or topographical photographs. At the time of painting the artist was living in Rome.

Spartali's oeuvre contains other Dantesque subjects, including *Dante and Beatrice on All Saints' Day* (Grosvenor 1881, unlocated), *A May Feast at the House of Folco Portinari, 1274* (Grosvenor 1887, Sotheby's 1984) and *At a Florentine Wedding Feast* (New 1890). On exhibition in 1888 the present work was accompanied by *Gelsomina* and *Mia Suora Rachel* (both unlocated), also from Dante, testifying to the artist's immersion in the poet's work at this period, through which she developed her distinctive aesthetic of figure groups and colour harmonies.

## 52 The Enchanted Garden of Messer Ansaldo
1889
s & d 'MS 1889'
watercolour and bodycolour on paper
72.3 x 102.8
Pre-Raphaelite Inc. by courtesy of Julian Hartnoll

This subject is from Boccaccio's *Decameron* (10th day, 5th story) which tells the story of Messer Ansaldo's love for Madonna Dianora, the virtuous wife of another man. With the aid of sorcery, he makes the garden blossom in mid-winter in order to win her. The scene shows him at his moment of triumph, hence the effective pictorial contrast between the warm air and spring flowers of the main composition and the snowy landscape glimpsed in the background, from which the ladies have just stepped in their fur wraps. The scene has an air of melancholy, however, since Dianora had no wish to see Ansaldo achieve the task, and is now torn between the desire to remain faithful to her husband and the obligation to honour her pledge.

Shown at the New Gallery in 1889, the work was dismissed by F.G. Stephens as "various pretty figures and fancies" (*Athenaeum*, 25 May 1889, 669). It re-appeared later the same year in the Liverpool exhibition, priced at £375.

The work's basic motif of a horizontal grouping in a garden builds on earlier pictures like *Tristram and Iseult* (1873, Sotheby's 1981) and *Fiametta Singing* (1879, Sotheby's 1975). The same year the artist also produced *The First Meeting of Petrarch and Laura* (1889, Sotheby's 1992). At this date she was painting with strong commercial purpose, despite generally feeling that her work did not meet the British public's taste. "I have sold in Florence and in Paris but very rarely in London," she told Brown (V&A).

Unlike Dante and Petrarch, Boccaccio was widely regarded as too bawdy for refined tastes. Here, the artist has chosen to downplay the sexual drama in favour of colour and decorative effect. Pictorially it reflects the 15th century art she studied in Italy, the page-boy figures in particular recalling Gozzoli or Ghirlandaio. It displays the unique look of her literary figure compositions, effecting a feminine version of late Pre-Raphaelite interests that may aptly be compared with De Morgan's *Garden of Opportunity* (1892, De Morgan Foundation). The present work may also have influenced J.W. Waterhouse's unfinished version of the same subject (Lady Lever Art Gallery).

## 53 How the Virgin Mary came to Brother Conrad of Offida and laid her Son in his Arms   1892
s & d with monogram and '92'
watercolour, bodycolour and gold paint on paper
49.5 x 80
Wightwick Manor, The Mander Collection (The National Trust)
Manchester and Birmingham showings only

Exhibited at the 1892 Liverpool Exhibition as *The Legend of Fra Conrado d'Offida*, this drawing shows the chief incident in the life of a Franciscan monk born near Ancona around 1240 and sanctified in 1817. Conrad's companion as he travelled the country was Blessed Peter of Treja, seen here watching from the edge of the wood. The model for Conrad is unidentified, but Peter is drawn from the artist's husband, W.J. Stillman. Subject and setting were supplied by the artist's long residence in Italy, seen here in the landscape background.

Spartali, who had previously ventured into the lives of the saints with the *Childhood of Saint Cecily* (1883 [fig.7]) followed the present work with another close in spirit, *The Vision of the Good Monk of Soffiano* (New, 1893, priv. coll.). Both contribute to the re-emergence of sacred subjects in this decade, seen also in work by Stokes [cats. 74 and 75], while the *Saturday Review* perceived in the *Vision*, "the tradition of Mr Madox Brown surviving in the work of the most intelligent if most mannered of his disciples," with a sincerity and piety of feeling that conveyed "some of the old Tuscan rapture." (13 May 1893, 511). Spartali returned to devotional themes with *Saint Francis Blessing the Pigeons he has Freed* (New, 1902, unlocated) and *Saint Catherine in her Garden* (1903, Manchester, unlocated).

Though Spartali is generally reckoned to have drawn from Florentine exemplars such as Giotto's frescoes of St. Francis, *Fra Conrado* bears a striking resemblance to Giovanni Bellini's *Assassination of Peter Martyr* (c.1510, National Gallery London), and to a version of it from the same date ascribed to the painter's workshop now in the Courtauld Institute Galleries. Closer in date, the subject has affinities with Burne-Jones' *The Merciful Knight* (1864, Birmingham Museum and Art Gallery) depicting an incident from the life of St John Gualberto. Spartali consulted Burne-Jones during progress on her work (see Marsh and Nunn, 1989, 106).

Priced at 170 guineas in 1892, the work was later acquired by Rosalie Mander from Chauncey Stillman, collaterally related to the artist's husband, who in 1970 recalled the magical impression its rabbits, forest, towers and haloed Madonna made on a child.

**54 St George** 1892
s & d with monogram and '92'
watercolour on paper mounted on panel
46 x 30.8
Delaware Art Museum. Gift of Mrs S.S. Auchincloss

This sensitive depiction of iconic manhood in the shape of the saintly knight - a figure familiar within Pre-Raphaelitism from the mid-1850s to the end of the century - was not exhibited during Spartali's life-time, and was given to an American friend, Wendell Garrison, editor of *The Nation*.

Popular with Victorian artists owing to his patriotic as well as religio-chivalric appeal, St. George is patron saint of both England and Greece, and thus doubly appropriate for the Anglo-Greek artist. The delicately-drawn youthful beauty of her hero expresses the purity and steadfastness of idealized masculinity, and compares well with Bunce's *Standard Bearer* from a similar date (cat. 71). The gentle tones underline Spartali's fine colour sense.

**55 A Florentine Lily**     c.1885-90
s with monogram
gouache and watercolour on paper
73.5 x 43.5
Private Collection

Exhibited at the New Gallery in 1895 but thought to have been painted some years earlier (Elzea 1989, 60), the title of this single-figure composition may be simultaneously interpreted as a young woman from Florence and the spirit of the city, whose fleur-de-lys emblem she holds and whose Palazzo Vecchio is seen through the window. Living and working in Florence from 1878-1885, Spartali retained an affection for the city. It has been suggested that the figure was drawn from a professional Italian model, though another possibility is the artist's daughter Effie, who was 20 in 1890 and at the start of her career in sculpture.

Offering a courtly counterpart to *Madonna Pietra* [cat. 50], it exemplifies the artist's treatment of one of the most consistent Pre-Raphaelite motifs, popular with both painters and patrons. Over the forty years of Spartali's career she made a distinctive mark in this mode, producing variations on the theme ranging from early works like *Mariana* [cat. 48] to *The Convent Lily* (1891, Ashmolean) and *Beatrice* (1895-6, Delaware) each endowed with colour harmonies and an individual earnestness that distinguishes them from more glib works in the genre by male artists. Comparable subjects in the exhibition are works by Sandys [cat. 30], Solomon [cat. 27], Zambaco [cat. 58] and Bunce [cat. 72], while the handling of a symbolic subject contrasts with Benham Hay's *England and Italy* [cat. 13]

# Maria Terpsithea Zambaco
## *née* **Cassavetti**

D.G. Rossetti, *Maria Zambaco,* 1870, Wightwick Manor, The National Trust, photograph courtesy of the Paul Mellon Centre for Studies in British Art

Born in London in 1843, the daughter of businessman Demetrius Cassavetti and his wife Euphrosyne, née Ionides, thus like Marie Spartali a member of the cultured, rich Greek community; her uncle Alexander Ionides was a renowned art patron in the 1870s. Having inherited a fortune from her father, in 1861 she married Demetrius Zambaco, a physician in Paris. She left him in 1866 to return with her son and daughter to London, where she began painting, probably under the instruction of Burne-Jones with whom she was romantically entangled around 1868-70. Another spell in Paris prefaced her return to London and adoption of sculpture as a student of Alphonse Legros, Slade professor and leading exponent of the art medal revival. Zambaco's first exhibited works were a terracotta bust of Legros and a head study (RA 1886, unlocated) followed in 1887 by a portrait bust and four medals presented by the artist to the British Museum [cats. 56, 57, 58]. In 1888, she showed two cases of medals at the New Gallery and 13 pieces in the Paris Salon. She also worked in plaster, participating in the 1889 Arts & Crafts Exhibition Society. A fervent admirer of Rodin, Zambaco returned to Paris in the 1890s, though little work of this date has come to light. Around 1906, she moved to Greece, and thence back to Paris, where she died in 1914. Although primarily known until lately as Pre-Raphaelite muse and "temptress", Zambaco began in the 1990s to be recognised as a versatile artist.

**56 Young Girl**   1885
s & d 'MDCCCLXXXV / M.T.ZAMBACO FECIT'
cast bronze
11.6  diam
Permission of the Trustees of the British Museum

The artist's first cast medal, this bears a portrait of an unidentified girl combined on the reverse with a decorative motif of three loosely entwined anemones. Exhibited at the Royal Academy in 1887, it was presented to the British Museum by the artist.

The absence of an inscription recording the name of the sitter may indicate that this was more of a prentice piece than a portrait. Modelled with engaging freedom, the work has been linked to the influence of early Italian examples in the British Museum by Antonio Pisanello, credited with inventing the genre in the 15th century, whose work was promoted by Alphonse Legros. In 1885 a competition for Slade student medallists organised by the Museum Keeper of Coins and Medals, stipulated that entries should have "on one side a portrait, and on the other some design illustrative either of the character, profession or life of the person portrayed." (quoted Attwood, 1992, 7). Although not registered at the Slade, Zambaco would seem to have taken up the challenge, working in a manner similar to the sisters Ella and Nelia Casella, who in 1885 exhibited medals (BM, see Attwood 1992) with illustrative reverses. The nymph Anemone was beloved of Zephyr and turned into a flower.

Zambaco's sitter may possibly be Marie Spartali's daughter Euphrosyne (Effie) Stillman, herself later a sculptor, who at this date was aged 13 and wore her hair in similar style. Female portraiture, especially of children and young girls, was often a woman artist's specialism, as for example Sandys' *Anna and Agnes Young* [cat. 32]

**57 Marie Stillman**   1886
s & d and inscr 'MARIE STILLMAN / MDCCCXXXVI / M.T. Zambaco'
cast bronze
13.5 diam.
Permission of the Trustees of the British Museum

This portrait medal of fellow artist Marie Spartali Stillman was exhibited at the RA in 1887 and presented to the British Museum by the artist. The reverse bears a madonna lily and "sine macula" - "without blemish" - the Latin epithet applied to the Virgin Mary, which is here used as a serious pun on the name and character of the sitter.

Derived via Alphonse Legros from Italian cast medals, this type of work represented a new departure in British 19th century art, harking back beyond the highly finished commemorative style of most Victorian medals to a more vigorous and expressive mode essayed by Pre-Raphaelite sculp- tors Woolner and Munro (see, for example, Barnes and Read, 143-8). This work has also been linked to 17th and 18th century medals such as that of Maddalena de' Medici by Antonio Selvi, with lilies on the reverse, which the artist could have seen in the British Museum (Attwood, 1986, 34). The combination of intimate portrait with symbolic flower imagery is seen elsewhere in Pre-Raphaelite practice, in the ubiquitous female heads with floral accessories.

Both sitter and artist were members of the Anglo-Greek community in London who became artists in their own right, but have largely been presented in histories of Pre-Raphaelitism as models and muses. The present work exemplifies the close personal relations between artists associated with the Pre-Raphaelite movement, and can be compared in this regard with the portrait sketches of Elizabeth Siddal by Howitt and Bodichon [cats. 2 and 5] and with De Morgan's portrait of Jane Morris [cat. 68] as well as offering an immediate comparison with studies of Spartali by Cameron [cat. 38].

### 58 Margherita di Prato    1886
d & inscr 'MARGH(E)RITA / DI PRATO / 1886'
cast bronze
12.0 diam. (uniface)

Permission of the Trustees of the British Museum

A third medal exhibited at the RA in 1887 and presented by the artist to the British Museum. Hitherto thought to be fictional, research sug-gests that Margherita di Prato is an historical figure from the trecento, wife of Francesco Datini, Prato's most illustrious citizen, whose house still stands in the city. Married in 1376, Margherita died around 1423. Her history was included in *Lettere di un notaro ad un mercato del secolo XIV,* (Florence, 1880). A later account describes her thus:

"From Margherita's letters a strong and simple character emerges. It does not, however, conform to either of the recognised feminine types of the period: she was neither Beatrice nor Griselda. We see a girl married at sixteen to a man already tired and soured, and who required from her, most of all, what she could not give him: a houseful of chidren ... but also a full-blooded and quick-tempered girl, bored and exasperated by her husband's nagging and his constant business worries, but making the best of a bad job ... and at last, when she had given up all hope of having a child of her own, agreeing to adopt and bring up her husband's bastard... A woman, who, as she grew older, showed herself as shrewd in business as her husband and an admirable housewife, fully capable of standing up to Francesco and of berating him soundly - and, in his last years, attempting more gently to lead him towards the pious thoughts which had become her own chief consolation." (Origo, 164).

If this is the figure depicted, she is shown as a young woman, garlanded with marguerites symbolic of her name. The historical subject, like Legros' medals such as *Maria Valvona* (1881, BM) pays conscious homage to Renaissance prototypes (Attwood, 1992, 14). While not keeping exclusively to female heads (her fourth RA exhibit in 1887 was a portrait of John Marshall, FRCS), Zambaco seems to have found them congenial subjects, rendered with pleasure rather than solemnity, in contrast to the "great men" favoured by Legros. Here the treatment is lively and expressive, with some of the feeling characteristic of the Pre-Raphaelite figure. The lyrical Italianate subject also compares with De Morgan's *Flora* [cat. 64].

# Francesca (Esther Frances) Alexander

*Francesca Alexander, age 80, photograph courtesy of Harvard University Press*

Born Boston, USA in 1837, the only child of portraitist Francis Alexander and a wealthy, religious mother. She was taught by her father after showing precocious talent. In 1853, the family moved to Italy, where they took up permanent residence, settling in Florence in the late 1860s. Between 1868 and 1882, Alexander gathered and made illustrations of numerous traditional hymns, stories and ballads of the region, producing pen and ink drawings motivated by a philanthropic notion of art's purpose and power. She did some oil painting between 1862 and 1878, though only four such works are presently known (e.g. *Woman Sewing*, 1860s, priv. coll.). In 1882 she was introduced to Ruskin, who became an admirer and ardent correspondent; he publicised her work in his lectures *The Art of England* in 1883, extolling the femininity of her work's minute and delicate style and compassionate sentiment. This led to the publication of individual drawings in the art press. Ruskin also assisted the publication in book form of *The Story of Ida* (1883), *Roadside Songs of Tuscany* (1885) and *Christ's Folk in the Apennines* (1888). In his enthusiasm for making Alexander's work more widely known, he bought the drawings for *Roadside Songs*, which had taken nearly fourteen years to complete, donating considerable numbers to the St. George's Museum in Sheffield and Oxford and Cambridge colleges. *Roadside Songs* was published in the USA as *Tuscan Songs* in 1897. Alexander's last publication, *Hidden Servants*, appeared in 1900. After her father's death in 1881, she looked after her mother, who died in 1916, leading a reclusive life despite her cult status. Her eyesight, which began to deteriorate in the mid-1880s, had gone completely by the time she died in Florence in January 1917.

**59. a,b,c,d Four Plates from Tuscan Songs (Roadside Songs of Tuscany)** 1868-82
pen and ink on paper
(a) 38.7 x 27.9; (b) 38.3 x 27.6; (c) 39 x 27.6; (d) 38 x 27.4
Ruskin Collection, Collection of the Guild of St George, Sheffield (a,b,c) and Birmingham Museums and Art Gallery (d)

These characteristic pages from Alexander's magnum opus *Tuscan Songs*, are four of 122, created over fourteen years. Of this delicate record of Tuscan culture, she said, "I have wished to make my book all of poor people's poetry... I have done my best to save a little of what is passing away". Though she meant to sell the completed work, it was not until Ruskin (introduced to the young American by her compatriot artist Henry Roderick Newman) enthused over her work that publication was proposed. After purchasing the manuscript in 1882, he selected 20 pages to be photographed by Frederick Hollyer (24 were reproduced in Ruskin's complete works, published 1906-12), and wrote a preface for the book which praised "the loveliness of the young and the majesty of the aged...the sanctities of mortal life [and] their traditions of immortality" that he found in Alexander's drawings (quoted Ruskin Gallery, 1992, 131).

(a) (plate VIII) depicts a scene from the story *The Madonna and the Rich Man*, acquired by Alexander from the shepherdess and improviser Beatrice di Pian degli Ontani. According to Alexander's own commentary, in this legend the Madonna, compassioning the lost state of the rich man, appeared to him in the form of a poor woman. The caption translates, "I have neither bread nor wine, what can I give you?".

(b) (plate XVI) shows a scene from *The Colonel's Leave*, where, having returned to his home town to pay his last respects to his dying sweetheart, the soldier pleads of her, "Speak to me, speak to me, little mouth of love".

(c) (plate XII), *The Jessamine Window*, shows another style of page found in the collection, in which the lyrics of a short song or rispetto are written out in both Italian and English, with the story illustrated on the facing page.

(d) carries the generic title *Rispetti*, and shows another song, included by Ruskin in an appendix as the last of 19 additional rispetti. Alexander's painstaking and fine style is exemplified in the use she makes of the flower referred to in each song as at one and the same time a decorative element on the page and a documentary aspect of her overarching project to record Tuscan culture. "On the hill of Bellosguardo, Alexander and his daughter on their walks were a familiar sight; she would stop from time to time and, under his guidance, draw the flowers or grasses with meticulous accuracy, as the peasants would gather round", writes Giuliana Artom-Treves (1956, 63). This harks back to Ruskin's vision of Pre-Raphaelitism, as well as evoking the long tradition of women as botanical illustrators.

Aided by Ruskin's promotion, especially in his 1883 lectures, *Roadside Songs* was a great success. Though Ruskin kept some of the drawings in his own possession, he had a characteristically didactic purpose in mind and distributed them amongst the St. George's Museum, Oxford University, Girton and Newnham Colleges Cambridge and Whitelands College Chelsea. Almost the entire work (108 illustrations) was published in the artist's native country in 1897 as *Tuscan Songs*.

# (Mary) Evelyn De Morgan *née* Pickering

Born 1855 in London, the eldest child of lawyer Percival Pickering QC and niece of middle-ranking Pre-Raphaelite painter J.R. Spencer Stanhope. She began lessons with a drawing master at age 15, followed by prize-winning studies at South Kensington and Slade Schools; in 1875 she paid her first visit to Italy. Her exhibition debut in 1876 at the Dudley Gallery with *St Catherine of Alexandria* was followed by an invitation to show at the Grosvenor Gallery, where she exhibited regularly (including sculpture 1880). In 1887 she married William De Morgan, ceramicist and associate of William Morris [cat. 63], with whom she shared a deep interest in spiritualism. From 1888 to 1901, De Morgan became a regular exhibitor at the New Gallery, establishing a reputation as an idiosyncratic artist in the van of Burne-Jones. Her preferred subjects included sacred and allegorical figures and scenes, and legends with a moral or social message such as *The Christian Martyr* (1882, South London Art Gallery) and *The Worship of Mammon* (1909, De Morgan Foundation), treated in a fashion that exploited her superior drawing skills and design sense, with striking colour and billowing draperies, often on a very large scale. From 1890-1914, for the sake of William's health, the couple divided their time between Chelsea and Florence; together they devised a painting method utilising glycerine which, though too troublesome to pursue, produced the clear, bright tones she sought. Her 1902 exhibition at Leighton House was followed by a solo show at Bruton Gallery (1906) and an exhibition of 25 works at Wolverhampton Art Gallery (1907). In 1916, her horror of the war led her to mount an exhibition of 13 works for the benefit of the Red Cross. De Morgan died in London in 1919, two years after her husband. Subsequently her brother and sister made arrangements for her works to be shown permanently, first at Leighton House and then Old Battersea House; now owned by the De Morgan Foundation, they form one of the largest existing permanent collections of work by a single artist in Britain.

*Evelyn De Morgan, photograph Courtauld Institute of Art courtesy De Morgan Foundation*

## 60 By the Waters of Babylon    1883
init & d 'EP 1882-83'
oil on canvas
89.5 x 166.7
De Morgan Foundation, London

The Biblical story of the exile of the Jews (Psalm 137) continued the interest in religious subjects the artist had shown throughout her first decade of work and was shown first at the Grosvenor Gallery of 1883 and illustrated by Henry Blackburn in his *Grosvenor Notes* for that year. It appeared later that year at the Manchester exhibition and again the following year at Liverpool.

This work may have been in part inspired by De Morgan's uncle Spencer Stanhope's *Waters of Lethe* (Manchester City Art Galleries) shown at the Grosvenor the previous year, though the presence of the American Kate Gardner Hastings' *By the Waters of Babylon* at the Grosvenor in 1883 suggests a general stimulus for this subject was in the air. An Italianate landscape personalises De Morgan's treatment, reflecting the several trips the artist had already taken to Italy since 1875 and leading to the judgement - not necessarily complimentary - that, "she looks at nature, whether in the human form or in landscape, more persistently than ever through the medium of the early Florentine School, illuminated by the sidelights of Mr. Burne Jones and Mr. Stanhope." (*Art Chronicle*, 1883,125). Evidently owing something to Burne-Jones (whose comparable *Mirror of Venus* had been a success at the first Grosvenor in 1877) but equally to Frederic Leighton, this impressive canvas attracted a range of critical opinion. In the words of the *Spectator* critic, " the picture is hardly rightly to be described as a failure, for it has, despite certain conventionalities of treatment and a too obvious echo of other artists' work, much truth of feeling, with considerable beauty of colour; the figures are well grouped and painted, the whole work is distinctly pleasant to look upon." (*Spectator*, 9 June 1883, 738).

Up to this point, De Morgan had divided her output equally between religious and mythological stories and characters and this was the last example of Biblical painting that she exhibited. Thenceforth she concentrated on mythological subjects. From this complex composition she took a number of elements for use in these subsequent dramas. The anguished female figure in the centre foreground was used again in several later works including the De Morgan Foundation's *The Valley of Shadows* (1899), *Boreas and the Fallen Leaves* (before 1907) and *The Death of the Dragon* (c.1916).

## 61 Dawn (Aurora Triumphans)    1886
init & d 'EBJ 1876'
oil on canvas
117 x 172.5
Russell-Cotes Art Gallery and Museum, Bournemouth

This painting, shown at the Grosvenor Gallery in 1886, is one of several based on the artist's belief in the symbolic dichotomy of light and darkness. The awakening of light - the drowsy figure at right - effected here by fanfares from heroic angel trumpeters, signifies enlightenment, and the driving away of darkness - the fleeing figure at bottom left - signifies the dispelling of the ignorance, doubt and bad faith that cloud the human spirit. Preparatory drawings indicate that the band of angels was the starting point and core image of the conception, which recent scholarship has linked to William Blake (Russell-Cotes, 1996), although an Italianate source observed during the artist's sojourns in Florence may well yet emerge.

The painting was offered for sale at the Liverpool Autumn Exhibition in 1891, after which it disappeared from De Morgan's exhibition record. At the beginning of this century, it was bought as a Burne-Jones masterpiece and was thus displayed in the collection of Herbert Russell-Cotes and his wife. The unsuspecting owners were apprised of this error when the artist's sister, Wilhelmina Stirling, recognised and correctly re-attributed the work at least twenty years after its purchase. The elaborate frame, too, had EBJ's name emblazoned upon it before Mrs Stirling's vehement intervention.

Today cat. 61 can be recognised as one of De Morgan's greatest works, utilising her favourite methods of allegory and symbolic figures, recurrent motifs such as the flying draped figure (seen also in *Night and Sleep*, 1878 and *Evening*

*Star Over the Sea*, undated) and the roped female figure (seen also in *Luna*,1885 and *The Valley of Shadows*,1899). Its characteristically bold scale shows how confidently the late-Victorian female artist was able to act.

**62 Medea**    1889
init & d 'EP 1889'
oil on canvas
149.8 x 88.9
Williamson Art Gallery & Museum, Birkenhead

On its exhibition at the New Gallery in 1890, this painting carried a quotation from William Morris' *Life and Death of Jason* (1867), "Day by day/She saw the happy time fade fast away/ And as she fell from out that happiness/ Again she grew to be the sorceress/ Worker of fearful things, as once she was". Forsaken by the calculating Jason, Medea turns once more to her magical powers for revenge, more in sorrow than in anger. She is dressed as a splendid queen in colours symbolising royalty and innocence, but her unhappiness is clear, suggested by the echoing marble halls through which she wanders. To counter her abandonment she turns to sorcery, the phial of poison meant for her rival Glauce smoking portentously in her hand. De Morgan rewrites the murderous mother of the classical world as a wronged woman whose magical powers should have attracted respect, not the cruel dismissal she received from the faithless Jason.

De Morgan utilises not only Morris' but also Ovid's characterisation of Medea, from *Heroides XII*, a source used by many contemporaries for a range of classical female figures including Penelope, Dido, Sappho and Ariadne (the subject of De Morgan's exhibit at the first Grosvenor Gallery [1877, De Morgan Foundation]). She had already treated the subject in a sculptured head, (1880) and made careful studies for this painting [fig.25]

From early in her career De Morgan had used this format of a long vertical containing a single full-length female figure (e.g. *Cadmus and Harmonia*, 1877, De Morgan Foundation), but this is the first of several sophisticated canvases in which she elaborates the settings and narrative contexts for these carefully selected heroines. The closest of these to the present work in purely visual terms is *The Thorny Path* (1897, Tatham Art Gallery, Peietermaritzburg). This sequence of figures shows the artist moving on from the work which may have been her chief original inspiration, Burne-Jones' *Hope* (1871, Dunedin Public Art Gallery) to the formulation of a gallery of female exemplars of the human spirit's trials and triumphs.

*Medea* went to the Liverpool Autumn Exhibition of 1890, and was sold from there to businessman Lewis Cohen, from whose estate it was bought in 1925 for the Williamson Art Gallery. A smaller pastel version is at Lanhydrock (National Trust, Cornwall).

**63 Portrait of William De Morgan**    1893
inscr, init & d 'William De Morgan / Florence 1893 / EDeM fecit'
oil on canvas
39.4 x 29.2
De Morgan Foundation, London

In 1887, Evelyn Pickering married the potter and eventual novelist William De Morgan (1839-1917), who is shown here looking improbably elfin at the age of fifty-four. He had begun in the 1860s as a designer in glass for Morris, Marshall, Faulkner and Co., but from about 1870 concentrated on ceramics. The De Morgans' partnership was what would be called nowadays a "companionate marriage" between two creative artists who felt themselves somewhat at odds with their families and time. They had no children, but pursued their professions and their shared belief in spiritualism with genuine, if eccentric, earnestness.

Not intended for exhibition, this portrait gives the artist's husband the look of a lightweight William Morris, direct and open-faced in his artist's smock. The small scale and plain handling offer a marked contrast to the flamboyance of Evelyn De Morgan's exhibition works of this decade such as *Medea*, *Flora* and *Earthbound* [cats. 62, 64, 66]. While portraiture plays a very small part in her oeuvre, De Morgan made a second likeness of her husband in 1909 (NPG).

Fig.25
Evelyn De Morgan
*Study for Medea*,
Private Collection,
photograph courtesy of
Sotheby's

**64 Flora**     1894
inscr init & d 'EDeM Maggio 1894'
oil on canvas
198.1 x 86.3
De Morgan Foundation, London

In 1890, the De Morgans acquired an apartment in Florence and began to spend half of each year there. This painting was made entirely in Florence and stands as a celebration of the city's early Renaissance artists whom the artist venerated, amongst whom Botticelli was supreme. It derives from studies that she made of Botticelli's great secular duo in the Uffizi Gallery, *Primavera* and *The Birth of Venus*, mediated through her study of Ovid's calendar of the months, the *Fasti* (see Gordon, 67-70). The goddess Flora, transformed from the nymph Chloris to be the Mother of Flowers, is introduced at the end of April. The artist makes both her sources clear in the figure's combination of Spring's and Venus' defining qualities and in the scroll at her feet, through which she addresses the viewer, or worshipper. It reads in Italian "I come down from Florence and am Flora/ This city takes its name from flower/ Among the flowers I was born and now by a change of home/ I have my dwelling among the mountains of Scotia/ Welcome and let my treasure amid northern mists be dear to you".

This painting was bought by one of De Morgan's few regular patrons, the Scottish shipowner William Imrie, who already owned *Gloria in Excelsis* (priv. coll.) and who was perhaps attracted by the reference within the figure's lore to his home country ("Scotia" was in general use for the North). He went on to commission other single full-length female figures, *The Undiscovered Country* (1894, Columbia Museum of Art), *Eos* (1895, Columbia Museum of Art), *The World's Wealth* (1896, priv. coll.), *Cassandra* (1898, De Morgan Foundation), and *Helen of Troy* (1898, De Morgan Foundation), which joined a collection containing works by Rossetti, Burne-Jones, Strudwick and Spencer Stanhope. All are founded on the earlier *Medea* [cat. 62], not only in the format but also in the fact that the same model

seems to have been employed for at least five of the paintings.

*Flora* was first brought to prominence by Walter Shaw Sparrow when discussing the artist's oeuvre in 1900. To exemplify her aesthetic, he wrote of "the presence of Botticelli's spirit, as in the quietly beautiful picture entitled *Flora*" (Sparrow, 1900, 227). Sparrow then used *Flora* to represent De Morgan's work in his book *Women Painters of the World* (1905). It remains much more famous than the work with which it can be compared most closely, the tapestry of the same name designed by Burne-Jones in 1885 (Exeter College, Oxford).

**65 Study for Earthbound**     c. 1897
chalk and gold paint on grey paper
29 x 36.5
De Morgan Foundation, London
on loan to The National Trust, Knightshayes Court

An inherent part of the Slade's training was the seriousness and industry displayed here, into which the earnest young Evelyn Pickering was happy to plunge. In 1874 she won four prizes, amongst them the First Certificate for Drawing from the Antique, while the prizes she won the next year included the Silver Medal for Drawing from Life. The meticulous preparation for figure subjects which was required and inculcated was premised on drawing, which De Morgan loved. Studies of limbs, gestures, the turn of a head and figural relationships such as the present one were made for each of her major paintings (see Russell-Cotes 1996).

**66 Earthbound**     1897
init & d 'EDeM 1897'
oil on canvas
87.6 x 118.1
De Morgan Foundation, London

Exhibited first in the artist's solo show at Leighton House in 1902, this allegorical composition is "where the artist tells what she thinks of the world's engrossing pursuit of wealth" (Sparrow, 1900). Thematically, it succeeds *The World's Wealth* (1896, priv. coll.) and anticipates *The Worship of Mammon* (1909, De Morgan Foundation).

Sparrow explained this work thus: "In a desolate country an aged king broods over his hoard of gold, while the dark Angel of Death approaches, a cloud-like mantle floating around her. It is strewn with stars, and a moon shines dimly in the angel's dusky wing, all typical of the elements into which the miser will soon be resolved. Away in the distance a freed spirit rises into the sky". When the painting was shown in 1907, De Morgan went further in her didactic intention in appending a verse of her own, adding to the clear anti-materialism of the subject her spiritualist beliefs concerning the temporary role of our physical form and the importance of transcendence towards a life hereafter: "Who clutches at a heap of gold/ Still clutches what he may not hold,/ The soul that knows no second birth/ Shall wane, fast held by Mother Earth./ Grim twins await his latest breath,/ Oblivion, hand in hand with Death:/ He sinks, the captive of his prize,/ Nor ever knows that others rise"

Though her style is completely different from that of G.F. Watts, the subject of *Earthbound* and related canvases has caused De Morgan to be linked to "England's Michelangelo", creator of such painted parables as *Mammon* (1884-5, Tate Gallery), *Hope* (1885-6, Watts Gallery), and *Love and Life* (1888-93, Louvre). The affinity should not, however, be assumed to have been one-way. Watts was known to be a great admirer of the younger painter.

### 67 Double studies of the Nude and Draped Figure
**(a) Female Figure**
black and white pastel on grey paper
42.5 x 61
De Morgan Foundation, London

**(b) Male Figure**
black and white pastel on grey paper
45.7 x 61.6
De Morgan Foundation, London

Study (a) is thought to be for the figure of an angel in *Attainment* (1900, destroyed) though the action is not identical. The bowed head and outstretched arms are a characteristic de Morgan action, seen also in the figure bending over a harp in *By the Waters of Babylon* [cat.60] and the angel in *Earthbound* [cat.66]

Study (b) is for the figure of a beggar stepping out of a boat in *St Christina Giving her Jewels to the Poor* (1904, destroyed)

De Morgan's careful and confident preparations for her imaginative compositions show the importance of the human figure in her conceptions. As a Slade student she was trained to make individual studies of each figure, first from life. Draperies might be studied separately before the two elements were brought together; heads, hands and feet were also often studied separately (see Russell Cotes 1996). Notably fewer studies exist of settings, revealing the weight put on the figure by the Slade method and the consequent significance of the School's provision of access to the life model for its male and female students.

### 68 Portrait of Jane Morris (Study for The Hour Glass) c.1904
coloured chalks on brown paper laid on canvas
46 x 35.5
De Morgan Foundation, London on loan to the William Morris Gallery, London

This careful head study of Jane Morris (1839-1914) is both a portrait and a preparatory work for cat. 69. "Mrs De Morgan painted Mrs Morris twice", reported her sister,"once in a fancy portrait entitled 'The Hour Glass', and once as an ordinary British Matron in everyday clothes" (Stirling, 1956, 138). This is the latter, though it might be disputed whether this iconic figure of Pre-Raphaelitism could be adequately described as an ordinary British matron. Contemporary photographs of William Morris' widow [fig. 26] confirm the peculiar charisma Jane Morris retained to the end of her life, as she outlived both the men who had brought her to prominence, her husband and Rossetti. The sitter had been a friend of the De Morgans for many years and they were at this period amongst her closest, most of her old associates being now dead.

Fig.26
*Portrait photograph of Jane
Morris*, c.1900,
William Morris Gallery,
London

Mrs Stirling went on to suggest that, "[t]o those who are familiar with the Rossetti portraits depicting her as an ideal Pre-Raphaelite beauty, with a long swan-like neck and masses of dark hair framing her exquisite face, these later, and possibly more realistic likenesses are of especial interest". There is an irresistible comparison to be made between the present work and cats. 2, 5 and 57, in which other Pre-Raphaelite icons, Elizabeth Siddal and Marie Spartali, shine through as individuals.

A full compositional study for the *The Hour Glass* in coloured chalks has recently come to light, showing the figure closely based on that of Jane Morris.

**69 The Hour Glass**     1905
init & d 'EDeM 1904-5'
oil on canvas
92.7 x 78.8
De Morgan Foundation, London

"Although at this time in failing health, Mrs Morris still retained her beauty and sat to my sister for a picture entitled *The Hour Glass* in which her handsome sombre face, with its haunting air of melancholy, was well adapted to the subject depicted", wrote Mrs Stirling some twenty years after the event.   "In an ancient chair, inlaid with ivory, a woman is seen seated.  Behind her on the wall are glowing tapestries; a gold lamp of medieval design is suspended above her head. Her draperies, in wonderful hues of yellow and russet bronze, are thickly sewn with pearls, the

delineation of which in correct perspective constituted a tour de force.  Jewels of barbaric design accentuate the richness of her attire and gleam again from her quaint head-dress, beneath which shows the first indication of age - her whitening locks.  Meanwhile, with a brooding sorrow her gaze is fixed upon an hourglass, clasped in her slender fingers, wherein the sands are swiftly running out; at her feet is a dying rose and close to her lies a book on which are visible the words *Mors Janua Vitae* (Death is the portal of life).  So, too, unheeded by her, outside the open doorway stands the figure of life the Immortal, piping, piping joyously in the sunlight in robes of azure amid the blossoming flowers of spring". (Stirling, 1924, p.215).

While traces of Burne-Jones' inspiration can, as usual, be discerned, *The Hour Glass* contains many characteristic De Morgan elements.  The striking quality of the figure's golden robe recalls the costumes of cat. 61's trumpeting angels and *Earthbound's* anti-hero, while the thematically enriching medievalised interior compares with those of *The Love Potion* (1903, De Morgan Foundation) and *Queen Eleanor and Fair Rosamund* (c. 1903, De Morgan Foundation).  A novel element was proposed by Mrs Stirling, when she declared that this painting was inspired by a movement of Beethoven's Waldstein Sonata (1805, opus 53), a composition generally more known for its heroic style and bold counterpointing of pace and mood than for any specific theme.

# Kate Elizabeth Bunce

*Kate Elizabeth Bunce,* from a family album, © Myra Kendrick

Born 1856 in Birmingham, the daughter of John Thackray Bunce, newspaper proprietor and chairman of the City Art Gallery. She was a prize-winning student at Birmingham School of Art in the 1880s, under principal E.R. Taylor and alongside her sister Myra Louisa Bunce (1854-1919) metalworker and watercolourist. Her first works seem to have been in the direct, well-drawn manner of the Birmingham School (her earliest known work is watercolour *The Sitting Room,* 1887, Birmingham City Art Gallery) but she was soon drawn to the Pre-Raphaelite mode represented by Rossetti and Burne-Jones (e.g. *How may I, when he shall ask?* RA 1887, unlocated; *The Keepsake,* 1901 [cat.73]), a manner seen to great effect in her most ambitious known easel painting, *The Chance Meeting* (1907, priv. coll.) [fig.5] , which depicts the encounter between Beatrice and Dante in the Vita Nuova. Bunce exhibited from 1887 to 1912 in Birmingham, Liverpool, Manchester and London. In 1893 she was among the artists invited to contribute to a sequence of historical pictures for Birmingham Town Hall (now lost). From 1888 an Associate of the Birmingham Society of Artists, she was also a founder-member in 1901 of the Birmingham-based Society of Painters in Tempera. Her two best-known works *Melody* [cat.72] and

*The Keepsake* [cat.73] chosen as "picture of the year" at the 1901 New Gallery, and her association with the Birmingham Arts & Crafts circle have led to Bunce's work being characterised as largely decorative, but her painting also displays strong figure drawing and moderated colour [cat. 70]. A devout Christian, she produced several works for churches, often in conjunction with her sister's metalwork. From around 1910 she concentrated on large-scale work for church interiors in Britain and Canada, comparable with that by Phoebe Traquair in Scotland. She died in 1927 in Birmingham.

**70 The Minstrel**   1890
s with monogram
oil on canvas
150 x 85
Private Collection

This painting's subject was described on its exhibition in 1890 as follows: "Through the narrow streets of a medieval town the glee-maiden pursues her way, touching her mandolin as she goes, self-absorbed and heedless of the gossiping remarks and the wondering glances of those who have clustered at their doors to see her pass" (*Birmingham Daily Post*, 19 September 1890, 4). A literary source can be assumed, though none was offered by this writer nor given in the catalogues of the two exhibitions where this work appeared in 1890, the Academy and the Birmingham Autumn exhibition. Complimented by the critic already cited as "a thoughtful production ... wrought out with genuine artistic feeling", *The Minstrel's* asking price of £60 shows that the artist considered it a major work. It is thought to have been bought by a local person, though information regarding Bunce's patronage is still very sparse.

The identification of *The Minstrel* and *The Standard-Bearer* [cat. 71] allows Bunce's development as a painter to be acknowledged for the first time in modern scholarship. Though there is a continuity of subject-matter in Bunce's entire oeuvre, she clearly formulated only in the last years of the century the highly decorative style, misleadingly called Rossettian, which characterises her better known works such as *Melody* [cat. 72].

**71 The Standard-Bearer**   1894
s with monogram
oil on canvas
77 x 46
Private Collection

Recently sold at auction as A Knight, this work is identified here for the first time as *The Standard-Bearer*, which appeared at the annual Birmingham Spring Exhibition in 1894 as Bunce's only exhibit. Thought to be a generic figure rather than the depiction of a particular saint or knight, it was received by the local press as "a dignified and well-composed presentation of an ideal personage in the picturesque ages of war. Evidently not a man who takes up his duties with a light heart or in a frivolous spirit, but one to whom the field of glory has tragic elements." (*Birmingham Daily Post*, 25 April 1894, 7). This composition employs the same model seen later in the figure of Dante in Bunce's *The Chance Meeting*, there given blonde hair, and introduces the eye-catching shield - possibly made by the artist's sister Myra, who is known to have collaborated with Kate as a metalworker in ecclesiastical paintings - which is also to be glimpsed in that painting, among the paraphernalia of the medieval merchant's bodega [fig. 5].

Though Bunce's many sacramental works frequently called, of course, for a male figure in the person of Christ (e.g. reredoses in St. Mary, Longworth, Oxon and St. Mary and St. Ambrose, Edgbaston, Birmingham), they were rarely as convincing as the present character, whose broad treatment emphasises the inherently romantic appeal the saintly knight had for Pre-Raphaelitism. Like Spartali's St George [cat.54] he stands as a late-century ideal of masculinity.

**72 Melody (Musica)**
c.1895
s with monogram
oil on canvas
76.3  x 51
Birmingham Museums and Art Gallery

Given to the City of Birmingham in 1897 by Sir John Holder, of Holder's Brewery, this painting has not so far been identified with any of the artist's exhibited works. In this light, and given that Sir John and Lady Holder were acquainted with the Bunce family, it can be surmised to have been a commission.

*Melody* builds on Bunce's Rossettian *The Daydream* (1892, unlocated) [fig.17], perhaps itself influenced by the Birmingham Art Gallery's acquisition in 1891 of Rossetti's *Beata Beatrix*, though more precisely reminiscent of his *La Pia de' Tolomei* (1868-80, Spencer Museum of Art, University of Kansas). The artist has, however, turned her back on Rossetti's sensual, suggestive approach and used a homely-faced model placed fairly and squarely in the picture-space while employing solid handling and bright, enamel-like colours. Though the

frontal image of a woman playing a lute-like instrument bears an obvious relation to the earlier *Minstrel* [cat.70], this is the first known example of the highly decorative style which came to characterise Bunce's later easel paintings, evident here in the vivid palette and the detail and variety of costume, textures and surfaces. The mirror, bowl and jewellery are of the style frequently exhibited by members of the Birmingham School, and may have been made by the artist's sister Myra.

The religious scene shown reflected in the mirror renders the figure's gaze one of pious contemplation and her absorption in the music she makes one of worship rather than sensuous gratification. This space-making device is typical of the increasing sophistication that *Melody* marks. This canvas displays vividly the intensity of the fin-de-siècle Pre-Raphaelitism which Bunce helped to develop.

**73 The Keepsake**  1898-1901
s with monogram
egg tempera on canvas
81.3 x 49.5
Birmingham Museums and Art Gallery

*The Keepsake* was chosen as "Picture of the Year" by the *Pall Mall Gazette* on its exhibition at the New Gallery in 1901. It illustrates D.G. Rossetti's pseudo-medieval poem *The Staff and Scrip* (1870), homing in on a passage after the death of the pilgrim "Then stepped a damsel to her side/ And spoke and needs must weep:/ For his sake, lady, if he died/ He prayed of thee to keep/ This staff and scrip".

The artist's cousin, Margaret Wright (later Chamberlain), who was staying with the Bunces during the second half of 1898, sat for the present work after - family tradition has it - the original model fell ill. In her unpublished diary, the visitor recorded: "Kate has asked me to sit for a painting so I went to her studio for two hours this morning. The picture is from the 14th century. In it I am the girl whose lover has been brought home from the battle field in fragments..." (20 September, 1898). Bunce proceeded steadily with the work, spending every weekday morning in the studio with her model. In February the following year, she reported to her cousin that a family friend, Katie Palmer, had sat for the head of the figure holding the staff on the extreme right. A further acquaintance, Ethel Newill, from another prominent artistic Birmingham family, was being sought for the remaining background figure. "I am painting the Queen's dress now and think it will come out all right", she concluded modestly (10 February 1899).

Why the work's exhibition appearance was delayed until 1901 is unclear, but the artist's sister Myra was able to write to their Canadian cousin in December that year, "I expect I told you how successful her pictures were last spring, especially The Keepsake for which you sat ... Lots of other places asked for the picture for their autumn exhibitions, but Kate had promised it to Birmingham, as it is her own town and she is an associate of the Society, so it has been here for this autumn exhibition" (15 December 1901). This was a triumphant return for Bunce to the Birmingham Society of Artists' bi-annual shows after a two-year absence. It was also shown in Manchester in 1903 (priced at £200) and at the Paris Société Nationale de Beaux-Arts in 1905, forming Bunce's only known exhibition appearance outside Britain in her lifetime.

Bunce was keenly interested in the revival of tempera as a medium for decorative painting, which was encouraged by Edward R. Taylor, head of the Birmingham Municipal School of Art from 1885 to 1903. She contributed work in this medium to the revival's first showing, at the New Gallery in 1901.

*Our thanks to M. Elaine Harvey for permission to quote from her grandmother's papers.*

# Marianne Stokes
## *née* **Preindelsberger**

Born 1855 at Graz, Styria in Austria, from whose art academy she won a prize enabling her to study in Munich, under von Lindenschmidt. A decline in family fortunes led to the professionalisation of her talent, and in 1880 she moved to Paris to attend the academies Trélat and Colarossi under Colin and Courtois, and also studied under Dagnan-Bouveret, a proponent of the "square brush" naturalism of Bastien Lepage. Her works in this mode were shown at the Salon (debut 1884) and RA (debut 1885). In 1883, painting in Brittany, a favoured location for plein-air artists, she met British artist Adrian Stokes (1854-1935) whom she married in 1884. They visited the Danish artists' colony at Skagen, and from 1886-1900 settled in St Ives, Cornwall, from where she exhibited regularly at RA, New Gallery, Institute of Painters in Oil and the annual Liverpool exhibitions. In 1893 she was awarded a medal at the Chicago World Fair art exhibition. In 1887 she and Adrian joined the progressive New English Art Club, and also visited Italy. This led to more

Hubert Vos, *Marianne Stokes*, 1890, unlocated, photograph University of Canterbury, NZ

147

imaginative subjects (e.g. *Aucassin et Nicolette*, 1900, Sotheby's 1994) and an interest in tempera. From the mid-1890s, Stokes moved steadily towards sacred subjects, of which *St Elizabeth Spinning for the Poor* [cat. 74] is a notable example, in conscious emulation of the spirituality and luminous colour she perceived in early Italian work. In 1899 the Stokeses went to the Netherlands and in 1905 paid the first of five visits to Hungary, which resulted in many paintings and a jointly-illustrated book, published 1909 in London. In 1910, Stokes exhibited in Budapest and in 1913 prints of her work were published by Hanfstangel in Munich, London and New York. In 1913-4, she and Adrian visited Sargent in Switzerland, returning to Britain after the outbreak of war. In 1923, she was elected Associate of the RWS. She died in London in 1927.

## 74 St Elizabeth of Hungary Spinning for the Poor
1895
s with monogram
oil on canvas
96.5 x 61
Private Collection

St. Elizabeth of Hungary, in the account most popular in 19th century Britain, was a medieval noblewoman canonised in 1235. Married at 14 to the landgrave of Thuringia, she was renowned for good works and self-mortification. After her husband's death, she refused to re-marry, renounced her coronet and became a nun. Here she is depicted as a young girl, her piety emphasised by the iconic head of Christ.

In Britain, Elizabeth's story was contested by low and high wings of the Anglican church, the latter promoting her as a model of Christian womanhood, the former using her celibacy to attack perceived Catholic proselytism. As a result incidents from her life featured in projected and planned works by several early Pre-Raphaelites, including a large oil by James Collinson (1851, Johannesburg Art Gallery), studies by Millais and Rossetti (see Tate Gallery 1984, 169) and a drawing by Charles Collins (1852, Tate Gallery). According to the *Art Journal*, Stokes, who as an Austro-Hungarian citizen presumably knew of the saint, took the subject from Wagner's *Tannhäuser* (1861). Her rendering is in telling contrast to Burne-Jones's *Laus Veneris* (Grosvenor 1878, Laing) which shares the same source, and

also to P.H. Calderon's erotically naked *Elizabeth* (RA 1889, Tate Gallery).

Exhibited at the New Gallery in 1895, *St Elizabeth* was the first picture by the artist "that aimed at both pure decoration and pure spirituality" (Magazine of Art, 1901, 243). It was executed during her stylistic conversion and shortly before she took to tempera for such subjects. Some pentimenti in the area of the arms in the present work indicate revisions of the pose. The treatment of head and hands recalls that of van der Weyden's *Magdalen Reading* (c.1440-50) in the National Gallery, where Stokes may have studied early art. The shallow space and flattened figure intriguingly recall one of the first Pre-Raphaelite works, Rossetti's *Girlhood of Mary Virgin* (1849, Tate Gallery) which itself re-appeared at the New Gallery in 1897.

*St Elizabeth* was exhibited widely, at Berlin in 1896 and Vienna in 1907, and remains with descendants of the original purchaser. In a second image of St Elizabeth (RA 1920, AG, New South Wales) she is an older woman sewing on an airy loggia.

## 75 Madonna and Child    c. 1907- 8
s with monogram
tempera on panel
80 x 59.5
Courtesy of Wolverhampton Museum & Art Gallery

Between 1905-10 the artist and her husband made several journeys to the Austro-Hungarian Empire, which resulted in a large number of paintings, an exhibition at the Leicester Galleries (1907) and the illustrated book *Hungary* (1909). One visit included the Austrian province of Dalmatia on the Adriatic coast (now Croatia) where the artist made a study for this work, showing a young woman in a red and blue cloak; called *Study for a Madonna (Dalmatia)*, this was included in the 1907 exhibition. With the addition of the Christ Child and symbolic briars arching behind, the present work developed, which may be identifiable as the *Madonna and Child* exhibited by Stokes at the Society of Painters in Tempera, 1909

(Baillie, no.3). A comparable unlocated work, *Madonna and Child with Symbols from a Litany,* was at the first show of the Society in 1905 (Carfax, no.14).

The highly wrought decorative effect of the thorns and embroidered bodice, together with the delicately painted muslin fabric and striking use of red, white and gold demonstrate the artist's skill in her chosen medium. In the words of the *Art Journal*, "Mrs Stokes unites perfect drawing with great sincerity and simplicity of painting, and her re-discovery of the gesso-grosso gives her a material and a method of singular directness and purity. What is done upon this ground, is done singly and at once; and it has a kind of daylight honesty and clarity which suit Mrs Stokes's learned simplicity and straightforwardness to great perfection ... She has done well to make this brilliant yet unsensational material her own." It added that tempera was especially appropriate "to the expression of Mrs Stokes's naive and, one may say, primitive temperament." ( 1900,1901).

The hieratic composition also contributes to the resurgence of Pre-Raphaelite interest in sacred themes in the final years of the Victorian era, while the depiction of the baby may be compared with the life studies by Boyce [*Sidney*, cat. 15] and Cameron [*Baby Pictet*, cat. 34] to emphasise the continuing and fundamental importance of nature to artists affected by the movement.

The work was given to Wolverhampton in 1930 by Sir Gerald Mander of Wightwick Manor.

## 76 Ehret die Frauen   1912
Tapestry. Wool and silk on cotton warp. Woven by Morris & Co.
174 x 256 cm
Whitworth Art Gallery, University of Manchester

"Honour to the women, they braid and weave heavenly roses into earthly life". The quotation in Gothic lettering along the top border is from Schiller's poem *Würde der Frauen (Woman's Worth,* 1796). Below, the figures are labelled left to right Courage, Caring, Love, Wisdom and Fidelity, each with appropriate attributes.

In the early 1900s, in hope of stimulating demand for tapestries at Morris & Co.'s Merton Abbey works, director H.C. Marillier commissioned new designs from "artists of the day", including Heywood Sumner and Byam Shaw. It may be that

by commissioning Stokes, the firm hoped to reach clients in Germany and Austro-Hungary sympathetic to the Arts & Crafts movement. In the event, the present tapestry was bought by a Morris client in Bognor, and acquired by the Whitworth in 1975. The cartoon was given by the company to Wixenford School chapel (Marillier, 36).

Though no previous connection between the artist and the Morris firm is known, there were mutual links with the Ionides family. Her design follows closely the Morris house style, especially as found in non-narrative pieces such as *The Orchard* (1890 from early designs by Morris) and *Angeli Laudantes* (1894 from a Burne-Jones design) where full length figures are placed against a verdure background. As with other Morris tapestries, J.H. Dearle contributed the foliage border design.

Owing to the archaic style and Germanic inscription, the result has been described as effective but "very old fashioned" (Parry, 124). The imagery loosely follows Schiller's text, a dual litany celebrating gender difference. Here the traditional, not to say conservative, qualities of womanhood honoured are those of fostering care (symbolised by the pelican); maternal love in the central Madonna figure; and teaching or wisdom (owl, lantern and hornbook). On either end are protective figures in armour and chainmail personifying courage and faithfulness. Though identified by Marillier as knights, some ambiguity of gender is visible in these beardless persons, pictorially suggestive of Joan of Arc.

149

# Christiana Jane Herringham
## née **Powell**

*Christiana Herringham, Collection of Mrs Vernon Jackson*

Born 1852 in London, the daughter of Thomas W. Powell, stockbroker and art collector. Her youth was spent mainly in Surrey as member of large (eight siblings) and wealthy family, from whom she inherited over £43 000 for her independent use. No details of formal art training are recorded, but she become a serious and well-respected copyist, specialising in early Italian works - a commitment which won the commendation of Ruskin. In 1880 she married Wilmot Herringham (1855-1936), a leading London physician knighted in 1914. Two sons were born, in 1882 and 1883; following the death of the elder in 1893, Herringham suffered a nervous collapse. Her new translation of Cennino Cennini's handbook on painting (published 1899 as *The Book of Art of Cennino Cennini, a contemporary practical treatise on Quattrocentro painting*), contributed to the revival of tempera techniques, in which she was a leading spirit. This interest was shared by Marianne Stokes and Kate Bunce. In 1905 and 1909 she exhibited in the Society of Painters in Tempera exhibitions. She was a founder member and first donor to the National Art Collections Fund (1903), working in conjunction with Roger Fry. Herringham was also on the organising committee of the National Union of Women's Suffrage Societies and a close associate of glass artist Mary Lowndes in this campaign. By 1909 she had a London studio and a country cottage in Buckinghamshire, where it is presumed she found the subjects of her large-scale nature paintings [cat.77-79]. From 1909 to 1911 she spent extended periods in India, tracing and copying the paintings in the Ajanta Caves, working with Dorothy Larcher, local assistants and William Rothenstein. On return to Britain she suffered mental delusions which permanently clouded her mind and closed her career. On Herringham's death in Malvern in 1929 her husband presented samples of her works to women's colleges in Cambridge and London.

**77 Foxgloves and Brambles**   c.1900-10
watercolour on paper
100.5  x 64.5
Lent by the Principal and Fellows of Newnham College, Cambridge.

So little is known of this artist's own painting that no firm dates can be attached to her large studies of wild flowers in their natural habitat. This, showing foxgloves and brambles in flower, suggests a woodland setting in late spring, somewhere in England. In the 1900s the artist and her husband had a cottage in the Chiltern woodlands of Buckinghamshire. However, early in 1909 she wrote to Will Rothenstein saying, "Next spring I think I shall stay some time at Burford and paint out of doors" (Lago, 175). If this plan was carried out, a setting in the Cotswolds is most likely.

Although practising chiefly as a copyist, the artist occasionally exhibited original, as yet unlocated, works with the Society of Painters in Tempera: *North Porch, Chartres* (1905 ), *In the Narthex of St Mark's, Venice* and *Florence from the Slopes of San Miniato* (both 1909). It may be that these prompted painting "from nature" in the English countryside. From 1910 the artist was occupied with her work at Ajanta.

In 1905 she wrote of the "wonderful luminosity" produced by tempera (Carfax, 6-7) and although in watercolour this quality is visible in the present work, where light shines through and on foliage. The careful delineation of nature in the wild demonstrates the application of Ruskinian principles in the manner if not the scale pursued by Brett throughout her career. "I believe the most beautiful position in which flowers can possibly be seen is precisely their most natural one ... All true lovers of art, or of flowers, would rejoice in seeing a bank of blossoms fairly painted; but it must be a bank with its own blossoms", Ruskin wrote in *Academy Notes* of 1857 (reprinted 1904: Cook and Wedderburn vol.14).

In 1917, after the onset of Herringham's dementia, her husband arranged for her works of art to go to institutions of higher education for women. This and cats 78-9 were thus given to Newnham College which in 1997 still admits only women students.

**78 Wild Clematis and Brambles**     c.1900-10
watercolour on paper
100.5  x 64.5
Lent by the Principal and Fellows of Newnham College, Cambridge.

This second exuberant study of nature in the wild, showing skeins of wild clematis in autumn, forms a pair with cat. 77 and suggests a sequence depicting the seasons.  A third work, described as "Bracken and other woodland foliage" (priv. coll.) may represent Summer.    Another, of different dimensions, showing wild narcissi, was bequeathed to Bedford College, London (now RHBNC).

The subjects compare with studies from nature by Brett [cat. 7] and Alexander [cat. 59]. The scale is striking, suggesting that Herringham was endeavouring to paint her woodland plants actual size.  In his *Academy Notes* of 1858 (reprinted 1904), Ruskin had chided Annie Mutrie for making "perfect dwarfs" of her foxgloves.  It is, however, difficult to imagine that pictures this size were painted al fresco.  The artist had a studio near her home in central London and it seems likely that her large flower paintings were scaled up from careful studies.

**79 Yellow Flags  [a] and [b]**     c.1900-1910
watercolour on paper
[a] 125 x 26.5
[b] 125 x 36
Lent by the Principal and Fellows of Newnham College, Cambridge.

Both decorative and botanically exact, these two tall flower studies from nature in the wild form a matching pair.  The tall narrow format corresponds with the yellow flag's actual size and shape. Clearly Ruskinian in inspiration, the works are comparable to wall paintings by Pauline Trevelyan and her guests at Wallington in Northumberland

(1855-8, National Trust). Presumably painted either in Buckinghamshire or near Burford [see cat. 77] they reflect the artist's love and knowledge of native British flora in outdoor habitat, linking them also to works by other "lady amateurs" like Edith Holden, artist of *The Country Diary of an Edwardian Lady* (1977).

*Our thanks to Dr Carola Hicks for bringing these works to our attention.*

# (Mary) Eleanor Fortescue Brickdale

*Eleanor Fortescue Brickdale in her Studio*

Born in 1872 in Upper Norwood (now south London), daughter of successful lawyer Matthew Fortescue Brickdale. She studied at Crystal Palace School of Art and Royal Academy 1897-1900. Her exhibition debut at RA 1896 was a black-and-white design, and her earliest work was in illustration, which remained a main aspect of her oeuvre. From 1899 she also exhibited large set-piece oils such as *The Pale Complexion of True Love* (RA 1899 [cat. 80]) in an eye-catching style, frequently with a sharp, almost satirical comment on conventionally romantic themes, recalling the early productions of Millais and Hunt. These became more flamboyant after the turn of the century (e.g. *Love and his Counterfeits*, RA 1904, Christie's 1996; *The Uninvited Guest*, RA 1906, [cat. 83]). From 1902 she had a studio in Kensington and pursued a dual career as painter and illustrator of fine colour-printed editions of literary texts such as Tennyson's *Poems* (1905) and Palgrave's *Golden Treasury* (1925); these being accompanied by regular exhibitions (at Dowdeswell and Leicester Galleries) of the original water-colours, of which a large number are extant [cats. 84 and 85]. Having personal connections with aviator Charles Rolls she took an interest in aeroplane technology, manifested in a large memorial picture to Rolls and *The Forerunner*, (1920, Lady Lever Art Gallery) depicting Leonardo da Vinci and his model flying machine. Brickdale was the first female member of the Institute of Painters in Oils, 1902, and a member of the RWS from 1903; she also taught for some years at the Byam Shaw School of Art. In later years her style broadened, and she also designed for stained-glass; a devout Christian, she also donated to churches (e.g. Lady Chapel triptych, All Saints, Newland, Glos.). In 1931 she was commissioned to paint *Ariel* for the BBC's Broadcasting House (untraced). Her professional career was closed in 1938 by a stroke, and she died in London in 1945.

## 80 The Pale Complexion of True Love    1899
s & d
oil on canvas
71.4 x 91.8
Private collection

"A lady exceeding fair, a lady sans merci who, habited in scarlet, submits with scant grace to the solicitations of an adorer, who, in his love-lorn subjection kneels to kiss the hem of her sumptuous garment" wrote the *Magazine of Art* critic of the artist's first major success, shown at the RA in 1899. (1902, 257)

The quotation (despite the attribution on the frame) is from *As You Like It*, Act III, when Corin speaks of Silvius' unrequited love for Phebe as "a pageant play'd Between the pale complexion of true love And the red glow of scorn and proud disdain". In using the motif, the artist set her theatrical mise-en-scène in a historical era more redolent of Renaissance Italy than Elizabethan England, and elevated her personages from Shakespeare's shepherds into the nobility.

Fig.27
J.E. Millais, *Lorenzo and Isabella*, National Museums & Galleries on Merseyside (Walker Art Gallery)

Brickdale began the work in 1898 with the £40 prize money she won in the RA Schools annual competitions for her design for an architectural decoration, *Spring*. Surprisingly, it appears to have attracted no immediate critical notice though it was illustrated in Blackburn's *Academy Notes* (1899, 38) and was sold from the Academy, together with the artist's other exhibit *That Overcometh the World* (unlocated ). It was also shown at the Liverpool Autumn Exhibition the same year.

This assertive composition recalls the vigorous figure pieces Millais produced in the first years of Pre-Raphaelitism, and may indeed represent conscious homage to the early Pre-Raphaelite involvement with English literature as a source of social drama. A work like *Lorenzo and Isabella* (1849, Liverpool, Walker Art Gallery)[ fig. 27], on show in the Millais retrospective at the RA in 1898, could have reminded Brickdale of the specific strengths of the tradition she was disposed to emulate.

### 81 The Ugly Princess    c.1902
s 'Eleanor F. Brickdale'
oil on canvas
91.5 x 51.4
Private Collection

This composition is inspired by Charles Kingsley's poem of the same name, whose concluding lines were quoted in the catalogue at its 1904 exhibition: "I was not good enough for man and so am given to God". The heroine is a princess forced to take the veil after rejection by her intended husband, presumably on the grounds of her deformity - Kingsley has her call herself "a dwarf". The artist shows her watching enviously as a pretty kitchen-maid and page dally in the yard below, before taking the step that will exclude her for ever from such pleasures.

This painting was first exhibited in March 1902 at the Society of Oil Painters, to which Brickdale had been elected the month before, the first woman to be thus acknowledged. It attracted favourable attention, described by the *Magazine of Art* as among "the best...most important figure pictures" (March 1902, 238) and used by the *Art Journal* to identify Brickdale as "one of the several followers of the Pre-Raphaelite school [represented here]". (March 1902, 92)

Apparently bought from exhibition by Gertrude Craig Sellar, widow of Scottish Liberal Unionist MP and landowner Alexander Craig Sellar, the painting was lent two years later to the artist's enormously successful solo exhibition - where all available exhibits were sold - at Leighton House. It was in Mrs Sellars' collection on her death in 1929 and has since remained in private possession.

*The Ugly Princess* can be related to the artist's black-and-white illustration of *King Cophetua and the Beggar-Maid* illustrated in the *Magazine of Art* in 1902 and thematically to the watercolour *Guinevere* [cat. 85], which shows another medieval noblewoman whom the (mis)fortunes of love bring to the convent.

### 82 The Little Foot Page    1905
s 'Eleanor F. Brickdale'
oil on canvas
91 x 57
Board and Trustees of the National Museums & Galleries on Merseyside (Walker Art Gallery, Liverpool)

The incident depicted is from the story of Burd Helen, the tragic heroine from Scottish balladry who dressed as a page to follow her cruel lover on foot while he rode on horseback. After bearing his child, she was finally acknowledged by him and they married. Helen is here shown secretly doffing her female attire and cutting her long golden hair, in preparation for her enforced journey.

While recalling Millais's *Ferdinand Lured by Ariel* (1849-50, Makins coll.) and *Ophelia* (1852, Tate Gallery), one of Pre-Raphaelitism's enduring romantic masterpieces, *The Little Foot Page* contrasts in all major respects with the other well-known Pre-Raphaelite treatment of this story, William Windus' *Burd Helen* (1856, Walker Art Gallery). It demonstrates W.S. Sparrow's claim that "[e]verything is well observed in her pictures, from the manner in which a tree's roots grip the earth to the most delicate tones of grey in a piece of rich drapery touched by sunlight" (*Studio*, 1901, 42). Like De Morgan's *Flora* [cat. 64], the full-length figure seems to be a celebration of the female artist's relatively recent access to the systematic study of anatomy and life-drawing. In this respect, it seems appropriate that a few years after this striking picture's exhibition, modern female art students in the capital were cutting their hair in 'page boy' style.

Surprisingly little is known about this work which, unusually, was not shown at the RA but at the Liverpool Autumn Exhibition in 1905. Brickdale may well have missed the sending-in date for the 1905 Academy, in overseeing the publication of her Tennyson's *Poems* and preparing a new series of watercolours for solo exhibition. The painting was purchased from Liverpool by Harold Rathbone and subsequently (1909) given to the city's collection, probably by Mrs Emma Holt.

*Our thanks to Edward Morris for assistance in compiling this entry*

**83 The Uninvited Guest**   1906
s 'Eleanor F. Brickdale'
oil on canvas
89 x 127
Private Collection

From 1901 to 1916, Brickdale showed one work a year at the Academy. *The Uninvited Guest* was her exhibit in 1906. A procession of richly-dressed people leaves a wedding ceremony, oblivious of the figure of Love, an "uninvited guest" at a marriage of rank, wealth and convenience in which sincere feeling has played little part. His pensive doubt fixes upon the bride, whose youthful, carefree joy is hindered only momentarily by the nettles and prickles growing beside the path from the church.

Two aspects of this composition attract particular attention: the virtuoso passage of the white satin bridal dress and the winged male nude. The first feature recalls not only the earlier daring of *The Pale Complexion of True Love* [cat. 80], but also Brickdale's continued admiration of Millais, whose *Black Brunswicker* (1859, Lady Lever Art Gallery) was noticed particularly for the cream satin dress

of its heroine. The second feature can be seen only infrequently in her painting, though it played a steady part in her illustrations, usually used poetically or whimsically. Brickdale always preferred to use the nude, as here, allegorically rather than naturalistically.

Like many of her allegorical or didactic compositions, *The Uninvited Guest* offers a moral homily for the present though set in past times. Introduced in watercolours such as *The World's Travesties* (1900, Christie's 1992) and continued in oils such as *The Deceitfulness of Riches* (RA, 1901, unlocated), the large-scale, ambitious composition with a serious message became Brickdale's chief preoccupation in the years before the war. The precise subject here, of true and false love, recurs in drawings and paintings, seen always not as a sentimental matter but as a question of honour. In their belief in the narratives of literature and history as the fittest source for moral guidance, such canvases as *The Uninvited Guest* represent the last glow of Victorian painting rendered inadequate by the unpredicted horrors of the war.

**84 I did no more while my heart was warm**
1908
36.5 x 25
pen & brown ink, water and bodycolours on paper
The Visitors of the Ashmolean Museum, Oxford

This is one of several designs after Robert Browning's poem "The Statue and the Bust" from his anthology *Men and Women* (1855), inspired by the imposing equestrian statue by Giambologna of the Grand Duke Ferdinand I in the Piazza della Santissima Annunziata in Florence that stands gazing towards the Riccardi-Manelli palace. Set in the upper classes of Renaissance Florence, the poem's story centres on a lady introduced on the eve of her marriage to a member of the Riccardi family who afterwards reveals himself a cruel despot. She falls in love with Duke Ferdinand, who returns her love, though their passion remains unspoken. She tries to glimpse her lover each day

from her turret window as he passes in the town square. This remains their only form of contact, since neither takes the initiative to further the romance. In despair at the passing of time and the continuing uselessness of her love, the lady commissions from the sculptor Andrea Della Robbia a bust of herself to set up at the window for her lover to see. In this act, she gives voice to the words of the title when, reflecting upon this unresolved passion, she says, "What matters it at the end?/ I did no more while my heart was warm/ Than does that image, my pale-faced friend". Brickdale's design perfectly captures the spirit of the lady's experience, with its vivid moment of longing and frustration, as she neglects her proper duties in the cause of a fruitless though all-too-human fantasy.

The Browning drawings appeared in Brickdale's 1909 exhibition at Dowdeswell's, after the publication of her illustrated edition of *Pippa Passes* and *Men and Women* (1908). This drawing, bequeathed to the Ashmolean by the artist's nephew, appears to have been omitted from both exhibition and book. As in her illustration to Cowley's poem [cat. 86], Brickdale has allowed herself to embroider the text. The poem makes no mention of the heroine becoming a mother during the course of her joyless marriage, but the artist's invention of the toddler presses home the poignancy of her situation.

There was early criticism that the subjects or stories of Brickdale's watercolour compositions were obscure. Perhaps her practice of adding to the textual references and her highly inventive compositions, so effective here, riled purists. They could have been especially disconcerted in this case that, though the artist depicts the key activity of the story - the heroine's eager gaze out of her window - she does so in a manner that robs the viewer of a sight of the fair face itself. Brickdale's interest in Browning, exhibited in earlier Pre-Raphaelitism by Boyce [cat. 17], Siddal [cat. 20] and Cameron [cat. 37], continued with the publication in 1909 of her illustrated edition of his *Dramatis Personae*.

**85 Guinevere**    1911
s initials
watercolour on paper
45.3 x 26.6
Birmingham Museums and Art Gallery

From 1901, Brickdale regularly exhibited watercolour sequences based on themes or texts which were then published as illustrated books. In 1911, the exhibition at the Leicester Galleries was based on Tennyson's *Idylls of the King* (first published 1859), already much illustrated (by Cameron among others: see *The little Novice and the Queen in the Holy House in Almesbury* [1874, University of Texas], with its similar personification of Guinevere). Brickdale depicted Guinevere, Arthur's Queen and lover of Sir Lancelot, a number of times in her career. Here, she reflects Tennyson's opening lines, spoken by the repentant Guinevere who has fled to a convent at Almesbury and asks to join the nuns so that she may "Walk your dim cloister, and distribute dole To poor sick people … And so wear out in almsdeed and in prayer/ The sombre close of that voluptuous day/ Which wrought the ruin of my lord the King". In Brickdale's illustrated edition of the *Idylls* published by Hodder & Stoughton (1911), this is the last plate, suggesting a resolution of the entire series as well as of Guinevere's own narrative. Brickdale chooses to show the queen in her repentant phase as a model of good womanhood - chaste, pious, obedient, philanthropic. This choice of exemplar compares with Stokes' nearly contemporaneous female imagery in *Ehret die Frauen* [cat. 76]. The nun had been a stock figure in Victorian art from the late 1840s, relating to debates about the role of both women and the church in modern society, as well as to the fashion for medievalism.

The work was bought on exhibition and presented anonymously to Birmingham the same year.

**86 Pride and Ambition here / Only in far-fetched metaphors appear**     1915
pen & brown ink, water and bodycolours on paper
36.6 x 25.2
The Visitors of the Ashmolean Museum

The title of this work comes from *The Wish* by Abraham Cowley (1618-1667), one of the verses illustrated by Brickdale in the sequence of watercolours based on *Old English Songs & Ballads* exhibited at the Leicester Galleries in 1915. Cowley's poem, recalling Horace's concept of the "beatus vir", is in praise of rural seclusion. The lines attached to this image are:

Pride and Ambition here
Only in far-fetched metaphors appear;
Here nought but winds can hurtful murmurs scatter
And nought but Echo flatter.

The protagonist shuns the meretricious attractions of court and city, preferring the quieter, profounder and more contemplative delights of rustic solitude. The peaceableness of this preferred world is emphasised by the view of the cultivated fields beyond the dwellings, the modest beauty of the domestic flowers and the companionship of the nicely observed cat (which the artist has introduced).

This design was reproduced as the seventh of 24 illustrations in the anthology *Old English Songs and Ballads* published in 1915.  It signals the enduring inspiration Brickdale derived from earlier phases of Pre-Raphaelitism in its echo of William Dyce's *George Herbert at Bemerton* (1861, Guildhall Art Gallery) and Brown's *Cromwell on his Farm* (1874, Lady Lever Art Gallery). Brickdale, like Dyce, suggests that the noble, sound spirit chooses the God-given delights of nature which will yield enduring pleasures not found in the ephemeral, brash gratifications of the man-made.  The message conveyed by Brickdale's rustic idyll harks back to the Ruskinian ethos of love of nature which reverberates throughout this particular collection of designs.  This idea was strongly to the fore in the early 1900s, as reflected in the work of the Georgian Poets, though mobilisation for the War in 1914-15 gives the theme a profound poignancy.

# Bibliography

**Books, articles, MS collections and abbreviations cited in the text, together with other works consulted.**

**Anderson**, Gail-Nina and Wright, Joanne, *Heaven on Earth : the Religion of Beauty in Late-Victorian Art,* 1994.

**Anonymous**, "Pre-Raphaelitism", *The Chromo lithograph,* 22 August 1868, 312-4.

**Anonymous**, "Edgbastonians past and present: Mrs Anna Blunden Martino", *Edgbastonia,* October 1898, xviii, no.209.

**Artom-Treves**, Giuliana, *The Golden Ring: the Anglo-Florentines 1847-1862,* 1956.

**Arts Council of Great Britain**, *Burne-Jones,* 1975.

**Attwood**, Philip, "Maria Zambaco : Femme Fatale of the Pre-Raphaelites", *Apollo,* July 1986, 31-37.

**Attwood**, Philip, *Artistic Circles: the Medal in Britain 1880-1918,* 1992.

**Baillie Gallery**, London, Exhibition of Society of Painters in Tempera, 1909.

**Barbican Art Gallery**, *The Last Romantics,* 1989.

**Barnes**, J. and Read, B., *Pre-Raphaelite Sculpture,* 1991.

**Bate**, Percy, *The English Pre-Raphaelite Painters, their Associates and Successors,* 1899.

**Birmingham Museums and Art Gallery,** *By Hammer and by Hand: the Arts and Crafts Movement in Birmingham,* 1984.

**Blackburn**, Henry, *Academy Notes,* 1899

**Bodleian Library**, MSS Department, Oxford.

**Brighton Art Gallery and Museum**, *Anthony Frederick Sandys,* 1974.

**BRP Papers**, Girton College, Cambridge.

**Burton**, Hester, *Barbara Bodichon,*1949.

**Carfax Gallery**, London, Exhibition of Society of Painters in Tempera, 1905.

**Casteras**, Susan P., *The New Path: Ruskin and the American Pre-Raphaelites,* Brooklyn Museum, 1985.

**Casteras,** Susan P., *Images of Victorian Womanhood,* 1987.

**Casteras**, Susan P., "Edward Burne-Jones and the Legend of Fair Rosamund", *Journal of Pre-Raphaelite Studies,* Spring 1988, 34-44.

**Casteras**, Susan P., *English Pre-Raphaelitism and its Reception in America in the Nineteenth Century,* 1990.

**Casteras**, Susan P. and Peterson, Linda H., *A Struggle for Fame: Victorian Women Artists and Authors,* Yale Center for British Art, New Haven, 1994.

**Casteras**, Susan P. and Denny, Colleen (eds.), *The Grosvenor Gallery: A Palace of Art in Victorian England,* Yale, 1996.

**Chadwick**, Whitney, *Women, Art and Society,* 1990.

**Cherry**, Deborah, *Painting Women: Victorian Women Artists,* 1993.

**Clayton**, Ellen C., *English Female Artists,* 1876.

**Cook**, E.T. and Wedderburn, A.,(eds.) *The Works of John Ruskin,* 39 vols., 1902-12.

**Crane Kalman Gallery** London / British Embassy Budapest, *Marianne and Adrian Stokes : Hungarian Journeys,* 1996.

**Crombie,** Theodore, 'Some Portraits by Frederick Sandys', *Apollo,* November 1965, lxxxii, 398-400.

**Delaware Art Museum**, *The Pre-Raphaelite Collection,* 1984.

**Dickens**, Charles, "New Lamps for Old", *Household*

*Words*, 15 June 1850, 265-7.

**Dixon,** Marion Hepworth, 'Our Rising Artists: Eleanor Fortescue Brickdale', *The Studio*, 1902.

**Doughty,** Oswald and Wahl, J.R., *The Letters of Dante Gabriel Rossetti*, 4 vols., 1965-7.

**E.B.,** "Madonna by Francesca Alexander', *The Magazine of Art*, 1889, 392-3.

**Edelstein**, Teri, "'The Song of the Shirt': the visual iconology of the seamstress", *Victorian Studies*, 1980, xxiii, 183-210.

**Elzea**, Rowland, "Marie Stillman in the United States: two exhibitions 1908 and 1982", *The Journal of Pre-Raphaelite and Aesthetic Studies*, Spring 1989, 56-72.

**Ford**, Colin, *The Cameron Collection*, 1975

**Fagan-King**, Julia, 'Cameron, Watts, Rossetti: the influence of photography on painting', *Journal of the History of Photography*, 1986, x, no.1, 19-29.

**Fitzwilliam Museum**, Cambridge, MSS Dept.

**Fredeman**, William E., (ed.), *The PRB Journal*, 1975.

**Frith**, William, 'Crazes in Art: Pre-Raphaelitism and Impressionism', *The Magazine of Art*, 1888, 187-91.

**Gaze**, Delia (ed.), *Fitzroy Dearborn Dictionary of Women Artists*, 1997.

**Geffrye Museum**, London, *Solomon: a family of painters*, 1985.

**Gernsheim**, Helmut, *Julia Margaret Cameron*, 1975.

**Gillett**, Paula, *The Victorian Painter's World*, 1990.

**Girton College**, Cambridge, *Barbara Bodichon 1827-1891 Centenary Exhibition*, June 1991.

**Gordon**, Catherine (ed.), *Evelyn De Morgan Oil Paintings*, De Morgan Foundation 1996.

**Haight**, G.S., *The Letters of George Eliot*, 9 vols., 1957-1978.

**Hamerton**, P.G., 'The Reaction from Pre-Raphaelitism', *Fine Arts Quarterly Review*, 1864, ii, 64-9.

**Harding**, Ellen (ed.), *Re-framing the Pre-Raphaelites*, 1996.

**Hardinge**, William M., 'A Reminiscence of Mrs W.M. Rossetti', *The Magazine of Art*, 1895, 341-6.

**Harrison**, Anthony H. and Taylor, Beverley (eds.), *Gender and Discourse in Victorian Literature and Art*, North Illinois University Press, 1992.

**Hasted**, Edward, *History and Topographical Survey of the County of Kent*, 1798, reprinted 1972.

**Herstein**, Sheila, *A Mid-Victorian Feminist: Barbara Leigh Smith Bodichon*, Yale University Press, 1985.

**Hopkinson**, Amanda, *Julia Margaret Cameron*, 1986.

**Howitt**, Anna Mary, *An Art Student in Munich*, 1853.

**Hunt**, William Holman, *Pre-Raphaelitism and the Pre-Raphaelite Brotherhood*, 1905.

**Johnson,** Barry C. (ed.), *Tea and Anarchy! The Bloomsbury Diary of Olive Garnett 1890-1893*, 1989.

**Johnson,** Barry C. (ed.), *Olive and Stepniak 1893-1895*, 1993.

**Kaplan,** Cora, *Salt, Bitter and Good*, 1975.

**Lago**, Mary, *Christiana Herringham and the Edwardian Art Scene*, 1996.

**"Lay Figure, The"**, "The Lay Figure and Pre-Raphaelitism", *The Studio*, 1898, xiii, 70.

**Macleod**, Dianne Sachko, *Art and the Victorian Middle Class: Money and the Making of a Cultural Identity*, 1996.

**Marillier**, H.C., *History of the Merton Abbey Tapestry works*, 1927.

**Marsh**, Jan, *Pre-Raphaelite Women; Images of Femininity*, 1987.

**Marsh,** Jan, *The Legend of Elizabeth Siddal*, 1989.

**Marsh,** Jan and Nunn, Pamela Gerrish, *Women Artists and the Pre-Raphaelite Movement*, 1989.

**McAllister,** Isabel, "In Memoriam: Evelyn De Morgan", *The Studio*, 1920, 28-9.

**Merritt**, Anna Lea, 'A Letter to Artists: Especially Women Artists', *Lippincott's Magazine*, (New York) 1900.

**Morris,** Edward, *Victorian and Edwardian Paintings in the Lady Lever Art Gallery*, 1994.

**Morris**, Edward, *Victorian and Edwardian Paintings in the Walker Art Gallery,* 1996.

**Newall**, Christopher, *The Grosvenor Gallery Exhibitions,* 1995.

**Newman,** Teresa and Watkinson, Ray, *Ford Madox Brown,* 1991.

**Nunn**, Pamela Gerrish, 'Ruskin's Patronage of women artists', *Woman's Art Journal,* 1981/2, ii, no.2, 8-13.

**Nunn**, Pamela Gerrish, 'Rosa Brett, Pre-Raphaelite', *Burlington Magazine,* 1984, cxxvi, no.979, 630-3.

**Nunn**, Pamela Gerrish, (ed) *Canvassing : Recollections by Six Victorian Women Artists,* 1986.

**Nunn**, Pamela Gerrish, *Victorian Women Artists,* 1987.

**Nunn**, Pamela Gerrish, "Artist and Model: Joanna Mary Boyce's 'Mulatto Woman'", *Journal of Pre-Raphaelite Studies,* new series II (2) Fall 1993, 12-15.

**Nunn**, Pamela Gerrish, *Problem Pictures,* 1995.

**Oliphant,** Dave (ed.), *Gendered Territory: Photographs of Women by Julia Margaret Cameron*, University of Texas at Austin, 1996.

**Oliphant**, Margaret, *Autobiography and Letters,* 1899.

**Origo**, Iris, *The Merchant from Prato,* 1957.

**Orr**, Clarissa Campbell (ed.), *Women in the Victorian Art World,* 1995.

**Parry,** Linda, *William Morris Textiles,* 1983.

**Peattie**, Roger, *Selected Letters of William Michael Rossetti,* Pennsylvania State University Press, 1990.

**Princeton**: Troxell Collection, Princeton University Library, New Jersey, USA.

**Quilter**, Harry, 'The New Renaissance; or, the Gospel of Insanity', *Macmillan's Magazine*, September 1880, xlii, 391-400.

**Robinson**, Annabel, Purkis, John and Massing, Ann, *A Florentine Procession,* 1997, Homestead Press, Cambridge.

**Rose**, Andrea, *Pre-Raphaelite Portraits,* 1981.

**Rossetti**, D.G. (ed.), *Early Italian Poets,* 1861.

**Rossetti**, D.G., *Poems*, 1870.

**Rossetti**, W.M., 'English Painters of the Present Day: Miss Spartali, the Junior Madox Browns', *The Portfolio*, 1871, 47-9.

**Rossetti**, W.M., *Dante Gabriel Rossetti: Family Letters,* 1895, 2 vols.

**Rossetti**, W.M., "Dante Rossetti and Elizabeth Siddal", *Burlington Magazine,* 1903.

**Rossetti**, W.M., *Some Reminiscences,* 2 vols., 1906.

**Ruskin**, John, *Lectures on Painting and Architecture: Pre-Raphaelitism,* 1854.

**Ruskin Gallery**, Sheffield, *Elizabeth Siddal - Pre-Raphaelite Artist,* 1991.

**Ruskin Gallery**, Sheffield, *Ruskin and Tuscany,* 1992.

**Russell-Cotes Art Gallery and Museum**, Bournemouth, *Evelyn De Morgan, Drawings and Paintings,* 1996.

**Shefer**, Elaine, "Deverell, Rossetti, Siddal, and the 'Bird in the Cage'", *Art Bulletin*, Sept. 1985, 437-448.

**Shires**, Linda (ed.), *Re-writing the Victorians: Theory, History and Politics*, 1992.

**Sellars**, Jane, *Women's Works,* National Museums and Galleries on Merseyside, 1988.

**Soskice**, Juliet, *Chapters from Childhood,* 1928.

**Sparrow**, Walter Shaw, "The Art of Evelyn De Morgan", *The Studio,* May 1900, 221-232.

**Sparrow**, Walter Shaw, *Women Painters of the World,* 1905.

**Stirling**, A.M.W., *William De Morgan and his Wife,* 1922.

**Stirling,** A.M.W., *Life's Little Day: Some Tales and other Reminiscences,* 1924.

**Surtees**, Virginia (ed.), *Sublime and Instructive,* 1972.

**Surtees**, Virginia, *Paintings and Drawings of Dante Gabriel Rossetti : A Catalogue Raisonné,* 2 vols., 1971.

**Surtees**, Virginia (ed.), *The Diary of Ford Madox Brown,* 1981.

**Surtees**, Virginia, *Rossetti's Portraits of Elizabeth Siddal,* 1991.

**Tate Gallery,** London, *An Exhibition of Paintings by Joanna Mary Boyce,* 1935.

**Tate Gallery**, London, *The Pre-Raphaelites,* 1984.

**Trevelyan**, Raleigh, *A Pre-Raphaelite Circle,* 1978.

**UT**: Humanities Research Center, University of Texas at Austin.

**V & A** : MSS Dept, National Art Library, Victoria & Albert Museum, London.

**Walker Art Gallery,** Liverpool, *Watercolours from the Walker,* 1994.

**Weaver**, Mike, *Julia Margaret Cameron 1815-1879,* 1984.

**West**, Shearer (ed.), *The Victorians and Race,* 1997.

**Whitworth Art Gallery**, *William Morris and the Middle Ages,* 1984.

**Yale**: Beinecke Rare Book and Manuscript Library, Yale University, New Haven.

**Abbreviations for exhibiting institutions and publications used in the catalogue section**

**RA** Royal Academy; **SFA** Society of Female Artists; **SLA** Society of Lady Artists; **BI** British Institution; **NI** National Institution; **SBA** Society of British Artists; **OWS** Old Watercolour Society; **RPS** Royal Photographic Society; **AJ** Art Journal.

# Photographic Acknowledgements

Photographic acknowledgements are due to the lenders and also to the following:

Christopher Wood, cat 3; Prudence Cumming Associates, cats 6, 8, 9, 14, 18, 23, 29, 32, 33, 38, 40, 41, 42, 43, 44, 45, 46, 47, 48, 81, 77, 78, 79, [a] and [b]; Rodney Todd-White and Son, 7; Comenos Fine Art, Boston, Mass., cat 13; Antonia Reeve, cat 17; Science and Society Picture Library, cats 34, 35, 37; Cliff Guttridge, cat 53; Bridgeman Art Library, cats 60, 63, 64, 65, 66, 67 [a] and [b], 68, 69; John Maclean, cats 70, 71; Magdalen Evans, cat 74; Sotheby's , cat 83, figs 1, 10, 15, 25; Christie's, cat 80; National Trust Photographic Library/ John Hammond, cat 28; Courtauld Institute of Art, cat 67 [a] and [b], fig 8; Rupert Maas, fig 2; University of Canterbury, N.Z., fig 4; Phillips Fine Art, figs 7, 16; Julian Hartnoll, cat 52, fig 9; Royal Photographic Society Picture Library, fig 13, Leger Galleries, fig 14, Frost and Reed, fig 5: RCHME ©Crown Copyright, fig 19; Pamela Gerrish Nunn, fig 17.